DINING AT GREAT AMERICAN
LODGES

SHARON O'CONNOR'S MENUS AND MUSIC

DINING AT GREAT AMERICAN LODGES

by

SHARON O'CONNOR

RECIPES FROM LEGENDARY LODGES
NATIONAL PARKS LORE & WILDERNESS LANDSCAPE ART
MUSIC BY THE BIG SKY ENSEMBLE

MENUS AND MUSIC PRODUCTIONS, INC.
EMERYVILLE, CALIFORNIA

Printed in Korea

Library of Congress Catalog Card Number: 2003106337
O'Connor, Sharon
Menus and Music Volume XVIII
Dining at Great American Lodges
    Recipes from Legendary Lodges
    National Parks Lore & Wilderness Landscape Art
    Music by the Big Sky Ensemble

Includes Index
1. Cookery 2. Entertaining
I. Title

ISBN 1-883914-35-3 (paperback with music compact disc)

Menus and Music Productions, Inc.
1462 66th Street
Emeryville, CA 94608
(510) 658-9100
www.menusandmusic.com

Book and cover design: Jennifer Barry Design, Fairfax, CA
Layout production: Kristen Wurz
Food photographer: Paul Moore
Food stylist: Amy Nathan
Prop stylist: Sara Slavin
Cartographer: Benjamin Pease

Artwork page 6: THOMAS HILL *Yosemite Valley* c. 1871
California Historical Society
Artwork back cover: CARL RUNGIUS *Lord of the Canyon* 1925
National Museum of Wildlife Art

10 9 8 7 6 5 4 3 2 1

BOOKS IN THE MENUS AND MUSIC SERIES

Holidays

Dinners for Two

Nutcracker Sweet

Music and Food of Spain

Picnics

Dining and the Opera in Manhattan

Lighthearted Gourmet

Rock & Roll Diner

The Irish Isle

Afternoon Tea Serenade

Spa

Bistro

Italian Intermezzo

Tasting the Wine Country

Museum Cafés & Arts

Dining at Great American Lodges

CONTENTS

INTRODUCTION   8

MUSIC NOTES   10

NATIONAL PARK LORE   12

HARVEY GIRLS   15

WPA AND CCC   16

MAP OF LODGES AND PARKS   18

BAR HARBOR INN   21
  ACADIA NATIONAL PARK   24

LAKE PLACID LODGE   31

GLENDORN, A LODGE
  IN THE COUNTRY   41

THE SWAG   51
  GREAT SMOKY MOUNTAINS
  NATIONAL PARK   53

CANOE BAY   61

CIBOLO CREEK RANCH   69
  BIG BEND NATIONAL PARK   71

THE HOME RANCH   79

THE LODGE AT VAIL   87

THE LAKE YELLOWSTONE HOTEL   97
  YELLOWSTONE NATIONAL PARK   99

JENNY LAKE LODGE   109
  GRAND TETON NATIONAL PARK   115
JACKSON LAKE LODGE   117

SUNDANCE   127

BRYCE CANYON LODGE   137
  BRYCE CANYON NATIONAL PARK   139

ZION LODGE   145
  ZION NATIONAL PARK   147

GRAND CANYON LODGE   153
  GRAND CANYON
  NATIONAL PARK   158
EL TOVAR   161

TIMBERLINE LODGE   169

THE AHWAHNEE HOTEL   179
  YOSEMITE NATIONAL PARK   181

FURNACE CREEK INN   191
  DEATH VALLEY NATIONAL PARK   193

THE LODGE AT KOELE   199

BASICS   210

CONVERSION CHARTS   218

CONTRIBUTORS AND
  NATIONAL PARKS   219

ACKNOWLEDGMENTS   220

INDEX   222

INTRODUCTION

Along with almost everyone else in America, I went through a period of reevaluating what was important in life after the shocking tragedy of September 11, 2001. After much consideration, I decided to begin a project that would celebrate one of the best ideas this country has ever come up with and an American original—our national parks. Thinking about national parks quickly led me to considering American lodges, delicious lodge cooking, and traditional American music.

I set off traveling across America to visit magnificent national parks and to stay in some of our country's greatest lodges. From a cook's point of view, I found an interesting mix of traditional cooking, regional foods, and cutting edge culinary trends at the lodges. From a musician's point of view, I decided to record historic, regional music in order to reflect our heritage and to have the tunes played in a way that would make them contemporary. I am forever grateful to musicians Peter Barshay and Jim Nichols for making my wish a reality. Staying at each of these lodges has been a great pleasure, but seeing the land around them has been pure joy. The past year has been filled with days in the wilderness, hikes and hot showers, fine dining and deep slumber, intense listening in the recording studio, much activity in my home kitchen, struggling to write the book, and experiences that need more superlatives than I can possibly come up with!

Enjoying an evening of fine dining at a classic lodge can create taste memories that last a lifetime. The recipes collected here are an eclectic, delicious mix. Some are flavorful regional classics, such as El Tovar's Black Bean Soup, and some are classic American comfort food such as blueberry pie from Bar Harbor Inn. Others reflect exciting innovation thanks to rising star chefs who are bringing sophisticated culinary interpretations to the countryside. At home, I suggest cooking with someone whenever possible—it's not only easier, it's also much more fun. We can enjoy each other's company while cooking, and when we're in the kitchen and sitting around the table we can make music part of everyday life. And of course the food tastes better because we've had a hand in making it. I've enjoyed cooking (and eating!) all the recipes in this book. I know you will enjoy making them in your own home kitchen.

While traveling to the lodges, I've been amazed by America's open lands. Our vast landscapes give me the feeling of freedom and a sense of limitless possibilities. One of the great American "inventions" of the nineteenth century was the idea that some land should be permanently protected for its natural value. This American concept has served as a model for park systems around the planet. Our parks have enjoyed good times and weathered bad times, and they are places where we can still go to remain connected to the land and to gather strength. These protected wild areas speak to the very core of our being. Our national love of independence, as well as our optimism, generosity, and deeply held respect for the land, are a legacy of our wide open spaces. These American traits were necessary for survival on the great American frontier, and vestiges of them are buried deep in the American psyche.

National parks give us a glimpse of our country's history and heritage. Children, parents, and grandparents can enjoy the parks together, and it's possible for a grandparent still to stand on a trail and say to their grandchild, "This is just the way it looked when I was your age." However, pollution, rising attendance, and shrinking funds are damaging the resources these places were set aside to protect. In order to preserve these treasures, our parks need everyone's help. As you check in at some lodges you can make a donation during registration, and at many parks you can join an association or an institute. If you would like to see more money going to the National Park Service, call or write your Congressperson. When visiting parks, my suggestion is to get out of your car as much as possible and get a feeling for the land. While working on this project, I met many national park service rangers and would like to acknowledge their dedication, knowledge, and good humor. Hopefully you will visit a park soon and meet some of these wonderful people.

In this book, I've included paintings by major wildlife artists and illustrators from the days of exploration and settlement to the present. Painters were instrumental in bringing natural wonders to the attention of the American public by portraying the marvels of this continent. Today, there are artist-in-residence programs at some of our national parks, and lodges such as Sundance and the Lodge at Koele foster artists so they can pursue their art and have a public forum to display it.

I'm extremely happy to have created the music CD that accompanies this book. The pioneers and settlers who ventured across our country brought with them remarkable and varied musical traditions, and the history of America is interwoven with their music. I hope the music captures the American spirit of openness and am glad the recording brings these tunes forward so we can keep enjoying them.

Creating this project has been a true joy and privilege. I have memories of lodges, landscapes, music, and a certain American way of thinking about our land. I'm left with small, deeply memorable moments—my glimpse of a grizzly bear through a spotting telescope, a close-up stare at spiky salt crystals in the middle of the desert, a green hike in the hills of Pennsylvania, feeling the enormity of the Grand Canyon, gasping at the beauty of the Grand Tetons, relaxing in the soft air of Hawaii, the fun of cooking the recipes with Lisa Donovan in my kitchen, and the joy of recording seven extraordinarily talented musicians.

I hope you'll enjoy making and serving these delicious recipes in your own home, love the music and play it frequently, and eventually visit all the lodges and parks. Since words represent shared memories, I hope you'll be able to do all these things so that we keep sharing the same memories. Don't miss the experience!

—*Sharon O'Connor*

MUSIC NOTES

Listening to the music CD that accompanies this book may awaken a memory of your elementary school, a summer campfire, or a country road trip. Millions of people across America have been united by some of these songs, all of which have outlived their initial burst of popularity while thousands of others vanished. These sentimental, tough, joyful songs have come down through the years, from generation to generation, and express part of what it is to be American. From a fiddler in a wagon train heading West to a jazz ensemble in the city, musicians have enjoyed making the tunes their own. Here, seven brilliant musicians ingeniously reinvent the songs, using their improvisatory imaginations to stretch boundaries. Some of the melodies are poignantly beautiful, while others swing like crazy in an unmistakably American way. Jazz musicians have always adapted great songs from different musical styles and used them as vehicles for improvisation. It's reassuring and enjoyable to hear tunes that have settled into the general treasury of American traditional music once again being brought to life. Recording the music at Fantasy Studios was fabulously fun, and it was an honor for me to work with guitarist Jim Nichols, pedal steel player Bobby Black, accordionist Rich Kuhns, violinist Chris Kranyak, pianist Michael Bluestein, drummer Paul van Wageningen, and bassist Peter Barshay.

"Shenandoah" was originally a ballad that told the story of a white trader who courted Shenandoah, the daughter of an Indian chieftain. He bore her away in his canoe across the wide Missouri. The melody later became a fine sea chantey that was sung by sailors as they worked turning a capstan, a shipboard apparatus around which cables are wound for hoisting anchors and lifting weights. "Buckeye Jim" is a haunting melody from the hills of Southern Appalachia. The simple song about a jaybird has an other-worldly beauty. "Wildwood Flower" is an old Civil War parlor song that was made popular by Mother Maybelle Carter, whose style of picking and strumming the guitar was influential in country music. The legendary Carter Family band often performed at the Grand Ole Opry, and Chet Atkins worked with them from 1948 to 1951.

The Big Sky Ensemble cuts loose with the infectiously rhythmic "Crawdad Song." A favorite in the South during the 1800s, this tune is about catching crayfish. "The Tennessee Waltz" was written by Redd Stewart and Pee Wee King and became a huge hit during the late 1940s and early '50s. In 1965, the beloved tune became the official song of the state of Tennessee.

After gold was discovered at Sutter's Mill in 1849, the migration from Pike County, Missouri to California was so immense that soon the word *pike* meant anyone from the Midwest on the road to California. "Sweet Betsy from Pike" was a favorite California immigrant song during the 1850s, and it was written, or put to paper and published by, John Stone in 1855. The melody is Irish and was probably brought to America by immigrants escaping the devastating potato famine. "Red River Valley" was originally a popular New York song, "In the Bright Mohawk Valley." The cowboys in Red River country changed the words, and the song became a favorite cowboy love song. "San Antonio Rose" was written by fiddle player, bandleader, and composer Bob Wills. The Texas Playboys, his legendary western swing band, made the tune popular during the 1940s.

When settlers first lived in Kansas, there were miles and miles between neighbors. In the evenings, people repaired tools, sewed quilts, and sang songs. In 1874, Dr. Brewster Higley, a farmer and doctor in Smith County, wrote the poem "Home on the Range" about the land, water, skies, and animals of Kansas. His neighbor, Daniel Kelly, wrote the music. "Home on the Range" is the state song of Kansas, and it was sung on the doorstep of Franklin D. Roosevelt's home by a group of newspaper reporters the night he was first elected President. "La Paloma" has been recorded by Charlie Parker, Elvis Presley, Dean Martin, and opera star Benjamino Gigli. It is difficult to find a person in the Western Hemisphere who hasn't heard this enduring melody. "Delicado" is by the Brazilian composer Waldyr Azevedo and was launched in the United States by Percy Faith, who recorded the tune in 1952. "Canadian Sunset," is by Eddie Heywood, a great jazz pianist who accompanied Billie Holiday for a number of years, and is a jazz standard that weaves the sound of romance. During the late 1920s and '30s, America was swept up with a fascination for cowboys and the romantic West. "Rye Whiskey" is a traditional tune that was recorded by the Sons of the Pioneers, a group that scored so many hits they became synonymous with Western music, sometimes called cowboy jazz. "Don't Fence Me In," composed by Cole Porter and based on a poem by Bob Fletcher, was meant for *Adios, Argentina* (1934), a film project that never made it to production. Roy Rogers and the Sons of the Pioneers sang the tune in the movie *Hollywood Canteen,* and in 1945 Roy Rogers sang the song in the movie *Don't Fence Me In.*

"Moe 'Uhane (Dream Slack Key)" is a tune that came to Sonny Chillingworth in a dream. Known as "the Waimea Cowboy," Chillingworth developed a melodic slack key guitar style that was influenced by Portuguese, Mexican, Spanish, and Polynesian songs. In slack key, a finger-picked acoustic guitar style that is unique to Hawaii, some of the guitar strings are slacked, or lowered, from standard guitar tuning. The roots of slack key can be traced to the 1830s, when the guitar was first brought to Hawaii by Mexican and Spanish cowboys hired by King Kamehameha to teach Hawaiian cowboys (*paniolos*) how to handle an overpopulation of cattle.

NATIONAL PARKS LORE

There can be nothing in the world more beautiful than the Yosemite, the groves of the giant sequoias and redwoods, the Canyon of the Colorado, the Canyon of the Yellowstone, the Three Tetons; and our people should see to it that they are preserved for their children and their children's children forever, with their majestic beauty all unmarred. —President Theodore Roosevelt

From Yellowstone's amazing geysers to the Grand Canyon's unsurpassed vastness to Yosemite's monolithic Half Dome, our national parks shelter the irreplaceable. The National Park System is founded on the belief that these landscapes belong to everyone, and enjoying them is a right that most Americans take for granted. Yet America's first European settlers came from a place where parkland belonged to the aristocracy, and penalties for trespassing were high. To people arriving from Europe, America's enormous stretches of land seemed dangerous, but also unclaimed—despite the fact that Native Americans had lived on this continent and tended its resources since prehistoric times.

Scientists and historians estimate that in the late 1700s there were about forty million buffalo on the American continent. Within a century, that number had decreased to barely one thousand. Buffalo were killed for sport, to feed crews working on Western railroads, and in an effort to destroy the livelihood of Native American tribes. In the 1830s, frontier artist George Catlin saw the destruction caused by westward expansion. Catlin wrote that wilderness, wildlife, and even native civilization could be preserved "by some great protecting policy of government . . . in a magnificent park . . . a nation's park." Within a few decades, Americans embraced the idea of national parks to protect landscape, wildlife, and history. Tragically, the conservation movement did not extend to saving Native American lives.

Throughout the 1840s and '50s, artists Thomas Cole and Frederic Church explored and painted on Maine's Mount Desert Island, now part of Acadia National Park (page 24). Their images inspired wealthy urbanites to visit the area in search of beautiful and inspiring scenery. For the American public, wilderness no longer seemed so frightening. Instead it was a destination, a place to find respite from the busy modern world.

One public figure who based his life's work on nature's power to heal and soothe was Frederic Law Olmsted, known as America's first landscape architect. Along with creating many of the urban parks we enjoy today, including New York City's Central Park, Olmsted drafted a bill to preserve Yosemite Valley. Although few Americans had actually seen the magnificent valley, public support for the bill was high. In Olmsted's report, famous landscape painter Frederic Bierstadt is credited with alerting Americans to the importance of saving Yosemite from uncontrolled development. Bierstadt, who had traveled west with explorer Frederic W. Lander, painted enormous, romantic, and very popular visions of a new Eden: the American West. In 1864, President Abraham Lincoln signed a bill granting Yosemite Valley and the Mariposa Grove of giant sequoias to the state of California to be "held for public use, resort, and recreation . . . inalienable for time."

Bierstadt's travels were not unusual, since landscape painters were often members of expeditions exploring new territories. Painter Thomas Moran, for instance, joined explorer John Wesley Powell in a journey over the Rocky Mountains. Moran's images of Yellowstone and the Grand Canyon captured the imagination of Americans and helped persuade members of Congress to create a park at Yellowstone. Wyoming and Montana were still territories, however, and Congress was unable to give the park to a state government. In 1872, Yellowstone became the first *national* park in the world.

Throughout the 1890s and the first decade of the next century, other parks were created by acts of Congress. President Theodore Roosevelt, who has been called the conservation president, was greatly influenced by a 1903 visit to Yosemite with renowned naturalist philosopher John Muir. In 1906, Roosevelt signed the National Monuments Act, giving the president power to protect important landmarks. In 1914, Secretary of the Interior Franklin K. Lane received a letter complaining about bad management in the parks. The letter was from Stephen Mather, a businessman who had made his

John Muir and Teddy Roosevelt in Yosemite, 1903

fortune in borax mining. Mather was a member of John Muir's Sierra Club (founded in 1892) and an avid outdoorsman. He was also a public-relations genius. Lane invited Mather to Washington to help persuade Congress that the national parks were in desperate need of their own governing agency.

Working with Horace Albright, a young lawyer from California, Mather realized that protecting natural resources could be profitable, thanks to the growing tourist industry. Since railroads offered the easiest way to visit the great parks of the West, he enlisted the help of railway executives interested in fostering Western travel. To convince politicians that America's scenic wonders were worth preserving, Mather organized camping trips through the great parks for prominent businessmen, writers, and politicians. These expeditions were brilliant examples of luxury in a rustic setting. Participants traveled between parks in specially outfitted Pullman cars and were served gourmet meals in the wilderness. A cook traveled with the party, and fresh produce was carried into the mountains by donkeys. Mather also hired Robert Sterling Yard to write *The National Parks Portfolio*, a lavishly illustrated description of the national park system. Financed partially by Western railroads, the portfolio was distributed to members of Congress and other influential Washington figures.

In 1916, several years of hard work and dedication paid off. President Woodrow Wilson signed the National Park Service Organic Act, creating a National Park Service (NPS) within the Department of the Interior. Mather was the first director of the new service, and Albright was assistant director.

The fledgling Park Service grew throughout the 1920s, as new parks were acquired. Although most early parks were west of the Rockies, many historic sites in the East were also added. Early on, Mather realized that park visitors would expect comfortable lodging and excellent food, even in rustic surroundings. A new style of architecture was created by Charles Whittlessey, Gilbert Stanley Underwood, Mary Jane Colter, and others. They used local materials and a building style influenced by European lodges, Western-style cabins, and Native American buildings. Many great lodges were financed by the railway industry, including Bryce Canyon Lodge (page 137), and El Tovar at the Grand Canyon (page 161).

During the Great Depression, the National Park System benefited from the Civilian Conservation Corps and the Works Progress Administration (page 16). More sites were added to the system until World War II brought decades of expansion to an abrupt halt. Throughout the war years, park service director Newton B. Drury successfully resisted efforts by industrialists who hoped to profit from park resources in the name of national defense.

By the late 1950s, after more than a decade of financial cutbacks, the national park infrastructure was in no shape to handle post-war tourism. Park visitation had increased from approximately six million in 1942 to thirty-three million in 1950. Conrad Wirth became director of the NPS in 1951, and his Mission 66 program set out to update park facilities by 1966, the fiftieth anniversary of the National Park Service. One of Mission 66's important goals was improved park visitor centers. With their audio visual exhibits and trained personnel, today's visitor centers are central to the park experience, helping guests interpret and enjoy the unique resources protected by each national park.

Prompted by concern that the growth of population and industry would leave no part of the United States untouched, Congress passed the Wilderness Act in 1964. Wilderness was defined as an "area where the earth and its community of life are untrammeled by man, where man himself is a visitor who does not remain." In the words of President Lyndon B. Johnson, who signed the act, "If future generations are to remember us with gratitude rather than contempt, we must leave them more than the miracles of technology. We must leave them a glimpse of the world as it was in the beginning, not just after we got though with it." Today, many of our national parks include official wilderness areas.

Throughout the 1970s and '80s, historic and recreation sites were added to the park system, as well as more than 40 million acres thanks to the Alaska National Interest Lands Conservation Act. During the 1980s and '90s, management companies restored and renovated significant buildings, such as the Lake Yellowstone Hotel, Jenny Lake Lodge, and El Tovar. National parks continue to be a favorite destination, and today's NPS administrators must balance the needs of park visitors with the protection of important resources. In 2002, more than 270 million people enjoyed our magnificent parks.

Thanks to the National Park Service, many of America's most important landmarks remain as glorious as they were hundreds of years ago. Hopefully, we will continue the long-standing tradition of protecting our parks for generations to come.

THE HARVEY GIRLS

Travelers today don't expect gourmet meals on the road or in the air. But our travel-fare is delicious compared to the greasy stews, biscuits like cardboard, and tasteless coffee served to railway passengers in the mid-nineteenth century. By the 1920's, an amazing change had occurred. When traveling by train to places such as Yellowstone and the Grand Canyon, Americans could expect excellent meals served by pleasant, intelligent women.

The story of the man behind this revolution is a typical American tale of immigrant success. Fifteen-year-old Fred Harvey came to the United States from England in 1850, and his first job was as a dishwasher in New York. By the time he died in 1901, Harvey owned a chain of restaurants, hotels, and gift shops that stretched from Chicago to San Francisco.

As a young man, Harvey worked his way up in the food trade and then went to work for the new railroad industry. After experiencing first-hand the indignities of dining in railroad depots, he inspired Charles F. Morse, head of the newly opened Atchison, Topeka, and Santa Fe line, with the idea of opening fine dining rooms across the west. The two men shook hands on the deal, and in 1876 Harvey renovated the lunch counter at the Topeka depot. The restaurant was an instant success, and Harvey opened another in Florence, Kansas (population 100), importing silver and crystal from England, Irish linens, and Konrad Allgaier, a fine chef from Chicago.

In the early twentieth century, waitresses were thought of as distinctly lower class. Fred Harvey made sure that "Harvey Girls," as his waitresses were called, were treated like professional women. Their demure uniform included a long black skirt, white apron, and neat bow tie. Harvey Girls lived together in dormitories under the watchful eye of a matron, and rules were strict. Despite long hours and rigorous standards, thousands of women saw waitressing for Harvey as an opportunity to earn a living and see the world. Many Harvey Girls went on to careers as nurses and teachers, and even more married a railway man, rancher, or local townsperson.

Soon, there were Harvey Houses all along the Santa Fe line, each organized so that a good meal could be served in the half hour allowed by the train stops. As tourism in the west increased, Harvey expanded his operations to include gift stores and grand hotels such as El Tovar at the Grand Canyon. Today, Harvey's legacy lives on, not only in the fast-food chains that live up to his standards of speed, if not quality, but in the fine lodging, food, and gift shops available to visitors at many of America's national parks.

THE WPA AND CCC

O n October 29, 1929, a massive stock market crash signaled the start of America's Great Depression, and by the early 1930s as many as one in four Americans were out of work. In 1932, Franklin D. Roosevelt won the presidential election with a campaign that pledged a "New Deal" for Americans. Among Roosevelt's reforms was a series of programs that provided meaningful work for the unemployed. Created in 1933, the Civilian Conservation Corps (CCC) hired millions of young men between the ages of seventeen and twenty-eight for conservation-related projects. The men worked in camps, many located in national parks. CCC projects included building roads, trails, bridges, and park buildings; restoring historic structures; reforestation; and even helping in natural disasters. The National Park Service was instrumental in organizing and administering the CCC.

Perhaps the most well known of Roosevelt's New Deal programs is the Works Progress Administration (WPA), established in 1935. Renamed the Works Projects Administration in 1939, the WPA employed more than eight million people before it was disbanded in 1943. Along with highway and building construction projects (Timberline Lodge, page 169), the WPA sponsored programs for unemployed artists, writers, musicians, and actors. Public buildings, such as post offices and schools, were decorated with murals, mosaics, and sculptures; community orchestras and choruses were organized; and writers traveled throughout the country completing state guides and collecting oral histories. Among the Federal Writers Project's important legacies are thousands of slave narratives: first-person accounts of slavery that would otherwise have been lost. Saul Bellow, John Cheever, Ralph Ellison, Zora Neal Hurston, and May Swenson are among the American writers who worked for the WPA.

The congressional mandate for the Federal Writer's Project was that workers completing state guides should "hold a mirror to America." Writers, musicians, photographers, and folklorists researched American folklore, recorded songs and stories, and studied folk art across the United States. Federal Music Program musicians were also hired to teach classes, perform in local symphony orchestras, and compose new works. Music, art, and oral histories from the WPA are available at the Library of Congress.

WPA artists produced posters on subjects ranging from public health to America's national parks. Richard Floethe, the New York supervisor of the Poster Division, had studied with Bauhaus painters Klee and Kandinsky. Floethe inspired artists to use bold colors, innovative lettering, and modernist design, helping to create the American modern art movement. WPA artist alumni include Jackson Pollock, Mark Rothko, and Louise Nevelson.

At a time when millions were in despair due to economic hardship, WPA artists documented and celebrated the daily experience of working people across the continent. In addition, Americans who had never before enjoyed live theater, heard a symphony orchestra, or seen fine art were given hope and inspiration by exposure to WPA plays, concerts, and artwork such as the posters on the following page. The WPA is a successful example of how artists and government can work together to enrich American lives.

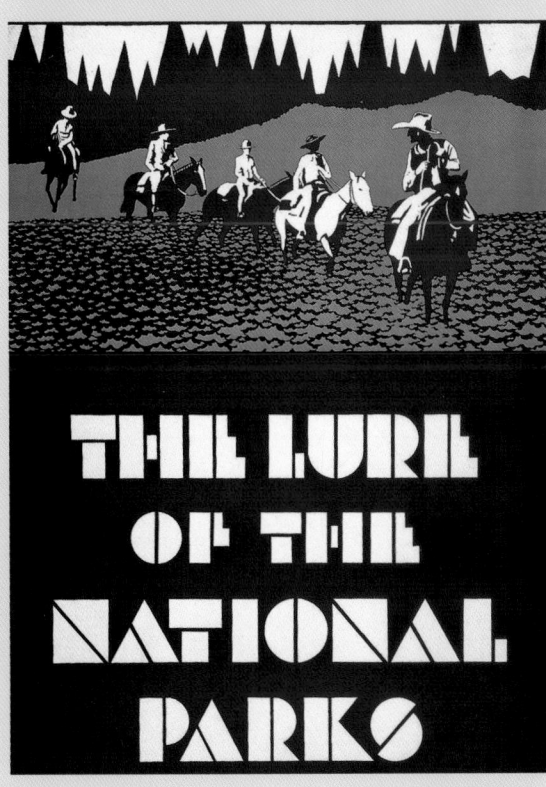

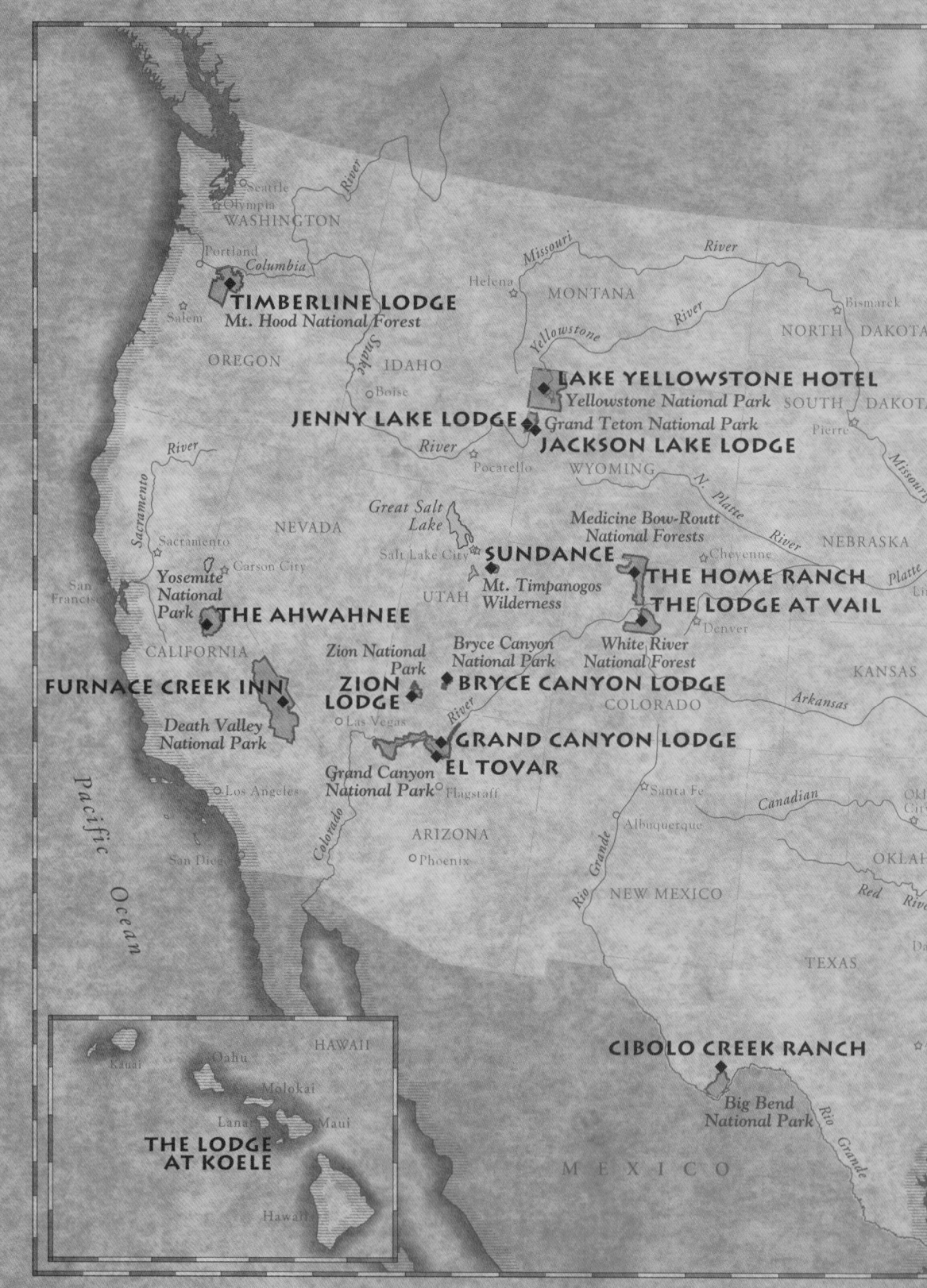

TIMBERLINE LODGE
Mt. Hood National Forest

LAKE YELLOWSTONE HOTEL
Yellowstone National Park

JENNY LAKE LODGE
Grand Teton National Park
JACKSON LAKE LODGE

*Medicine Bow-Routt
National Forests*

SUNDANCE

THE HOME RANCH
THE LODGE AT VAIL

*Mt. Timpanogos
Wilderness*

THE AHWAHNEE

*White River
National Forest*

*Zion National
Park*
*Bryce Canyon
National Park*
**ZION
LODGE**
BRYCE CANYON LODGE

FURNACE CREEK INN

*Death Valley
National Park*

GRAND CANYON LODGE
EL TOVAR
*Grand Canyon
National Park*

CIBOLO CREEK RANCH

*Big Bend
National Park*

**THE LODGE
AT KOELE**

CANADA
Gulf of Saint Lawrence
St. Lawrence River
MAINE
BAR HARBOR INN
Augusta
Acadia National Park
Adirondack Park
LAKE PLACID LODGE
VT.
Montpelier
NH
Concord
MA
CT
Connecticut River
Hudson River
Albany
NEW YORK
Lake Ontario
Allegheny National Forest
GLENDORN
PENNSYLVANIA
New York
Harrisburg
NJ
MD
Washington D.C.
Lake Superior
Lake Michigan
Lake Huron
Lake Erie
Ice Age National Scenic Trail
CANOE BAY
WISCONSIN
Madison
MICHIGAN
Lansing
Mississippi
IOWA
Chicago
Moines
River
ILLINOIS
Springfield
River
OHIO
Columbus
Indianapolis
INDIANA
WEST VIRGINIA
Charleston
River
Ohio
Wabash
Frankfort
Richmond
VIRGINIA
KENTUCKY
Jefferson City
MISSOURI
Tennessee
Great Smoky Mountains National Park
Charlotte
NORTH CAROLINA
Raleigh
Nashville
River
THE SWAG
TENNESSEE
SOUTH CAROLINA
Columbia
Little Rock
River
ARKANSAS
Atlanta
Savannah River
Birmingham
Chattahoochee River
MISSISSIPPI
LOUISIANA
Jackson
ALABAMA
GEORGIA
Jacksonville
Mobile
Tallahassee
Baton Rouge
New Orleans
FLORIDA
Tampa
Miami
Gulf of Mexico
Atlantic Ocean
N
E
S
W
0 Miles 800
0 Kilometers 800

BAR HARBOR INN

BAR HARBOR, MAINE

An elegant seaside resort with a storied past, Bar Harbor Inn overlooks Frenchman Bay on fabled Mount Desert Island. Within two miles of Acadia National Park, the inn is an ideal base from which to explore the park. Bar Harbor Inn enchants visitors with its historic elegance and offers many opportunities for culture, recreation, and relaxation.

In the late 1800s, two Hudson River Valley School artists, Thomas Cole and Fredric Church, visited Mount Desert Island, and the magical landscapes and seascapes

> **MENU**
>
> *Lobster Pie*
>
> *Roast Pork Loin with Sweet Potato and Corn Hash*
>
> *Blueberry Pie*

they painted became fashionable in East Coast homes. Those who admired the artwork soon wanted to visit Mount Desert Island for themselves. Although early visitors stayed in local taverns and with farmers and fishermen, by the 1870s there were at least sixteen hotels in Bar Harbor, many of which were booked two years in advance. By the end of the 1800s, the Astors, Rockefellers, Carnegies, Vanderbilts, and other wealthy industrialists of the Gilded Age had built the elegant summer showplace homes that were euphemistically known as "cottages."

The first social club to be organized on Mount Desert Island was started in 1874 and named the Oasis Club. The exclusive men's club moved into quarters known as the Mount Desert Reading Room in 1887, with the avowed purpose of promoting "literary and social culture." The club's handsome cedar-shingle building was designed by architect William Randolph Emerson, and it is still enjoyed today as part of Bar Harbor Inn. The club was a center of social activities during the summers before the first World War, and President Taft was entertained there in 1910 during his stay at Bar Harbor. For the next thirty-five years, the club flourished, and its ranks swelled with visiting yachtsmen and officers of the U.S. Navy. Women were allowed admittance only by invitation on special occasions, but in 1921 they started to enjoy equal status with men at the club. In that same year, a restaurant was opened to the public and the club sought more investors because of increasing maintenance costs. By 1922, the club was no longer financially feasible, and it was sold to the

Maine Central Railroad. Until World War II, the building had a variety of tenants, and during the war the Navy used it as an observation headquarters.

In 1947, a catastrophic fire raged through Bar Harbor, destroying over 250 showplace homes as well as hotels and other buildings. The Mount Desert Reading Room was used by the American Red Cross while giving assistance to many who were burned out. After the fire, Bar Harbor was left without a single hotel, and in 1950 a group of townspeople joined together to develop the Hotel Bar Harbor. David J. Witham purchased the property in 1987 and changed its name to the Bar Harbor Inn. By 1998, Witham had completely redeveloped the property into an elegant oceanfront resort.

Bar Harbor Inn is situated on a promontory at the head of picturesque Frenchman Bay. The inn has eight acres of lush lawns and gardens, and three separate buildings house its 153 comfortable guest rooms, many with fireplaces and balconies that overlook the ocean. The Main Inn has a large elegant lobby with a fireplace, guest rooms and suites, and the historic Reading Room Restaurant.

Guests can relax on the spacious grounds, take walks on the town pier, or stroll along the Shore Path with views of the Porcupine Islands and historic shorefront "cottages" from

Bar Harbor's Gilded Age. They can also go for a sail on Frenchman Bay aboard the *Margaret Todd*, Maine's only four-masted schooner, which docks at the inn's private pier. There are daily commercial and Acadia National Park–sponsored interpretive cruise excursions from the pier to outer islands and lighthouses, as well as whale watch, schooner, nature, or deep-sea-fishing cruises. Four scenic golf courses are nearby. The Arcady Music Festival, Bar Harbor Music Festival, and the Acadia Repertory Theater are some of the cultural activities to take in during the summer.

Bar Harbor Inn's Reading Room Restaurant has been welcoming guests since 1887, and it is a delightfully elegant place to enjoy fine dining with gorgeous views of an active commercial harbor. Many of the boats in Frenchman Bay catch lobsters, and the restaurant's menu features a traditional Maine lobster bake, lobster bisque, and the delicious lobster pie on page 26. Every evening during the season, performances by a pianist or classical harpist set a romantic mood during dinner. Executive chef Lou Kiefer, who has more than twenty years experience in Maine's coastal kitchens, created the following recipes.

ACADIA NATIONAL PARK

MAINE

A magical cluster of islands off the Maine coast, Acadia was the first national park established east of the Mississippi. Although it is one of the nation's smaller national parks, encompassing about 47,000 acres, it receives over three million visitors a year. Bounded by the sea, Acadia includes much of Mount Desert Island, the Schoodic Peninsula, and several off-shore islands.

Deep shell mounds indicate there were Native American encampments in the region dating back about 6,000 years, but prehistoric records are scarce. The Wabanaki people were living in the region when the first European explorers arrived and called the island Pemetic, or *Sloping Land*. In 1604, the explorer Samuel de Champlain landed on the island and named it Isles des Monts-Désert: Mount Desert Island. In his journal, he noted that the "mountain summits are all bare and rocky." The land was claimed by the French, then by England, and finally by the United States.

By the early 1800s, farming, lumbering, fishing, and shipbuilding were major occupations for the region's American settlers. Visiting landscape painters of the Hudson River School, including Thomas Cole and Frederic Church, glorified the island during the mid-1800s and inspired visits by city dwellers. These "rusticators" came in the summer to savor fresh salt air, the area's natural beauty, and the relaxed pace. Mount Desert became a summer retreat for the Rockefellers, Vanderbilts, Carnegies, Astors, and other wealthy industrialists during the 1880s and the Gay Nineties. They built showplace family estates euphemistically called "cottages," but the Great Depression and World War II curtailed their extravagance. In 1947, a huge fire burned 17,000 acres near Bar Harbor, consuming many of the great houses as well as 10,000 acres of Acadia National Park.

Although the extremely wealthy used the Bar Harbor area as a summer playground, they also had a lot to do with preserving the region. George B. Dorr, who came from this social strata, devoted forty-three years of his life, energy, and family fortune to protecting the landscape. Dorr established a corporation whose sole purpose was to preserve land for perpetual use by the public, and acquired 6,000 acres that he offered to the federal government. In 1919, President Wilson signed an act that established Lafayette National Park, which was renamed Acadia in 1929. Dorr became the park's first superintendent.

Many national parks were established to high-light and protect a specific natural feature. Acadia's natural beauty, however, interweaves magnificent ocean shoreline, granite-domed mountains, deep forests, freshwater lakes and ponds, and lovely meadows. Massive geologic forces formed the land-scape over great expanses of time, and persistent forces of erosion, such as water, wind, and waves, continue to slowly shape the parkland today. Rocky slopes rise above the shore, including Cadillac Mountain, which at 1,530 feet is the highest point on the East Coast. In addition to Acadia's spruce–fir forests, there are stands of deciduous maple, birch, and beech that turn a brilliant mix of red, yellow, and orange in the fall. The foliage begins to turn in September and is usually at its peak during the first two weeks of October.

A hiker's paradise, Acadia has more than 120 miles of hiking trails that range from easy to strenuous. Forty-five miles of rustic carriage roads weave through the landscape for bicyclists, walkers, and joggers. The roads were built between 1913 and 1940 by John D. Rockefeller, Jr., and are the best examples of broken-stone roads in the United States. Carriage rides are available at Wildwood Stables, and for automobile drivers, the park's twenty-seven-mile Park Loop Road introduces many scenic natural attractions.

Between mid-May and mid-October, National Park Service rangers lead interpretive walks, talks, and cruises to an offshore island. Whales, harbor seals, bald eagles, peregrine falcons, and ospreys can be sighted, along with occasional glimpses of beavers, foxes, moose, and puffins. Many park visitors bring their paintbrushes and easels or their cameras.

In this place of spruce-fir forests, cool ocean breezes, and quietude for the contemplation of sea, shore, and sky, visitors have found simple pleasures and unsurpassed loveliness for more than a century.

FREDERIC EDWIN CHURCH *Sunset* 1856 Munson Williams Proctor Arts Institute

Down on the shore we have savored the smell of low tide—that marvelous evocation combined of many separate odors, of the world of seaweeds and fishes and creatures of bizarre shape and habit, of tides rising and falling on their appointed schedule, of exposed mud flats and salt rime drying on the rocks.

—Rachel Carson

LOBSTER PIE

These individual lobster pies can be the first course for a special dinner, or a supper in themselves when served with crusty bread and a green salad. Lobster conjures up visions of Maine with good reason: The state's catch supplies 90 percent of the nation's lobster supply.

$1^1/2$ pounds cooked lobster meat,
  coarsely chopped
$3/4$ cup ($1^1/2$ sticks) unsalted butter
2 cups heavy cream

1 cup dry sherry
2 cups crushed oyster crackers
2 teaspoons sweet Hungarian paprika
4 teaspoons unsalted butter, melted

✿ Preheat the oven to 350°F. In a large frying pan, melt the butter over medium-high heat and sauté the lobster for 1 or 2 minutes. Pour in the sherry and stir to scrape up any cooked bits on the bottom of the pan; remove from heat.
✿ In a medium saucepan, simmer the cream until reduced by almost half. Remove from heat and sir in the lobster mixture. Pour into 4 casseroles or ramekins. In a small bowl, combine the cracker crumbs and paprika. Sprinkle the crumb mixture over each lobster pie and drizzle with melted butter. Bake in the preheated oven for 15 minutes, or until the mixture bubbles at the sides.
Makes 4 servings

ROAST PORK TENDERLOIN
WITH SWEET POTATO AND CORN HASH

Lean but tender pork tenderloin, served on a bed of colorful hash.

MARINADE
$1/2$ cup olive oil
6 garlic cloves, minced
3 tablespoons minced fresh thyme
Salt and freshly ground pepper to taste

One 2-pound pork tenderloin,
  trimmed
1 tablespoon olive oil
Sweet Potato and Corn Hash
  (recipe follows)

In a medium bowl, combine all the marinade ingredients. Add the pork tenderloin, cover, and refrigerate for 24 hours, turning occasionally. Remove from the refrigerator 30 minutes before cooking.

Preheat the oven to 350°F. Heat a large ovenproof frying pan over medium-high heat for 60 seconds. Add the olive oil and heat until almost smoking. Add the pork tenderloin and brown on all sides. Transfer the pan to the oven and roast for 15 to 20 minutes, or until an instant-read thermometer inserted into the thickest part of the meat registers 160°F. Remove from the oven and cover loosely with aluminum foil. Let stand for about 10 minutes.

To serve, cut the pork into thin slices. Place a mound of sweet potato and corn hash in the center of each of 4 warmed plates. Arrange slices of pork around the hash and serve at once. *Makes 4 servings*

SWEET POTATO AND CORN HASH

2 large sweet potatoes, peeled and
    finely diced
Kernels cut from 2 ears fresh corn
2 tablespoons olive oil
1 small red onion, finely diced

1 red bell pepper, seeded, deribbed,
    and finely diced
1 tablespoon *each* minced fresh thyme,
    basil, and rosemary
Salt and freshly ground pepper to taste
2 tablespoons dry white wine

Cook the sweet potato in salted boiling water for 3 minutes. Add the corn kernels and cook for 2 minutes; drain.

Heat a large frying pan over medium-high heat for 60 seconds. Add the olive oil and heat until almost smoking. Add all the hash ingredients except the wine and sauté until the potatoes begin to brown, about 7 minutes. Pour in the wine and stir to scrape up any browned bits from the bottom of the pan. Serve the hash hot. *Makes 4 servings*

BLUEBERRY PIE

A classic American pie to serve with vanilla ice cream or fresh whipped cream.

PASTRY

2 1/4 cups all-purpose flour

1/2 teaspoon salt

1/2 cup (1 stick) cold unsalted butter,
  cut into small pieces

1/4 cup vegetable shortening

4 tablespoons water

FILLING

5 cups fresh wild Maine blueberries or
  fresh or frozen blueberries

1/2 cup sugar

1 1/2 tablespoons flour

3 tablespoons cold unsalted butter,
  cut into pieces

1 egg yolk, lightly beaten

3 tablespoons sugar blended with
  2 1/4 teaspoons ground cinnamon

In a food processor, combine the flour, salt, butter, and vegetable shortening and process until the mixture resembles coarse crumbs, about 15 seconds. With the machine running, add the water and process until the dough begins to form a ball, about 20 seconds. On a lightly floured surface, form the dough into a ball. Divide the dough in half and flatten each piece into a disk. Cover with plastic wrap and refrigerate for at least 1 hour.

Preheat the oven to 450°F. On a lightly floured surface, roll out 1 pastry disk to a 12-inch-diameter round. Fit into a 10-inch deep-dish pie pan. Trim the dough, leaving a 1-inch overhang. Roll out the top crust.

In a large bowl, combine the blueberries, sugar, and flour. Pour the mixture into the prepared pie shell, mounding slightly. Dot with butter, cover with the top crust, trim the edges, fold them under, and crimp. Brush the crust with the egg, sprinkle with the cinnamon sugar, and cut 3 or 4 steam vents. Bake in the preheated oven for 10 minutes. Reduce the temperature to 350°F and bake for 50 minutes, or until the crust is golden brown. Let cool before cutting into wedges. *Makes 1 pie*

LAKE PLACID LODGE
LAKE PLACID, NEW YORK

MENU

Salad Composée

Roast Duck Breast
with Black Pepper Curry

Crème Brûlée

Set in the heart of Adirondack Park, a six million-acre preserve deemed "forever wild" by the New York state constitution, Lake Placid Lodge is a sumptuous lakefront retreat. The romantic hotel looks out over the water to Whiteface Mountain, sight of the 1932 and 1980 Winter Olympics. Both rustic and splendid, the inn is a member of the prestigious Relais & Chateaux organization. Created in the spirit of the Great Camps, it is a sophisticated, luxurious place hidden away in quiet woods.

For more than a century, the timber of the Adirondacks has been protected from being sold, removed, or destroyed. It is America's largest state park, bigger than Yellowstone, the Grand Canyon, and Yosemite combined! Beginning in the 1880s, millionaires of the Industrial Age built their lavish summer retreats, known as the great camps, and trainloads of city dwellers came to rough it every summer. The main building at Lake Placid Lodge was one of those old camps, and when David and Christie Garrett discovered it, they were determined to return the lodge to its classic heritage and recreate the original atmosphere. Today their extensively renovated lodge is furnished with the country's largest collection of true Adirondack furniture, all of which is designed and made by local master artisans.

Lake Placid Lodge includes seventeen rooms and suites and seventeen snug cabins at the water's edge. Public rooms in the main lodge are filled with art, antiques, and Oriental rugs, and fireplaces are always burning. Guests can retreat to the cozy pub, relax in the game room, or sit in stout wicker chairs on the wide porch overlooking the serene glittering lake and the mountains beyond. The supremely comfortable guest rooms are individually decorated with rustic twig and birch bark furniture, rich fabrics, featherbeds, and stone fireplaces. The cabins are grouped along the forested edge of the lake. These thick-walled homes in the woods have beamed ceilings, Adirondack-style four-poster beds, walk-in closets, luxurious bathrooms with deep tubs, and warming stone fireplaces.

Lodge guests can enjoy outdoor activities year-round. On the lake, they can cruise in nearly silent electric boats, glide out in a canoe, or set sail in the lodge barge for a sunset cruise around the lake. There is lake swimming and basking on a sandy beach, as well as fishing. In fact, the 32-pound trout caught in Lake Placid in 1985 was the largest lake trout taken in the continental United States since 1919! Guests enjoy hiking or mountain biking on trails through forests of balsam, spruce, pine, and birch. They can join a guide to explore a remote area where moose, wild turkeys and black bears roam free, or they can choose to play golf on the eighteen hole golf course or tennis on one of the four courts that are just steps away. In winter, cross-country skiing or snowshoeing along Jack Rabbit trail is an exhilarating way to earn a hearty evening meal. At Lake Placid village there is indoor

and outdoor ice skating and exciting downhill skiing at Whiteface Mountain. The lodge is only a short drive from the village of Lake Placid, where boutiques, galleries, restaurants, and antique shops abound.

Food is a focal point at the lodge, and here world-class dining has a distinct Adirondack flair. Breakfast offers a bounteous buffet with freshly baked breads, muffins, smoked fish and meats, cheese, and omelettes. In the evening, the dinner menu brings sophisticated city fare to the country

and features chef Sean Mohammed's contemporary world cuisine. His fabulously innovative menus change with the season and use organic local products whenever possible. Marvelous private dinners are served in the wine cellar, and the restaurant's wine list has received Wine Spectator's "Best of Award of Excellence." On most evenings, candlelight and crystal are set out on the twig-framed porch facing the glorious view, and guests can dine at twilight to the lulling of waves in the lake. After dinner, a fire blazes on the shore where s'mores are toasted and brandies sipped. Chef Sean Mohammed created the following recipes and presented them to Menus and Music.

The Adirondacks remain a real wilderness, and at this extraordinary small hotel it is possible to enjoy warm hospitality and privacy in a glorious lakefront hideaway where time passes, cares cease, and a magical calm descends.

We need the tonic of wildness. This curious world which we inhabit

is more wonderful than it is convenient, more beautiful

than it is useful—it is more to be admired and enjoyed then, than used.

In wildness is the preservation of the world.

—Henry David Thoreau

LAKE PLACID LODGE

SALAD COMPOSÉE

A luxurious first course. The lime-soy vinaigrette is sensational on any green salad.

4 quail eggs

BLACK PEPPER CRUST MARINADE
2 tablespoons cracked black peppercorns
2 tablespoons sweet soy sauce* or
   regular soy sauce
2 tablespoons soy sauce
1 tablespoon minced peeled fresh ginger
1/2 shallot, minced
1 garlic clove, minced

4 large shrimp, shelled and deveined
1 tablespoon olive oil
Lime-Soy Vinaigrette (recipe follows)
6 large handfuls baby salad greens
4 thin slices chilled foie gras,**
   optional
4 thin slices smoked salmon
4 thin slices prosciutto
Freshly grated coconut or unsweetened
   shredded dried coconut for garnish

🌿 Put the quail eggs in a small saucepan and add water to cover. Bring to a boil over medium heat, reduce heat, and simmer for 7 minutes. Remove the eggs and run them under cold water. Let cool, then peel and set aside.

🌿 In a medium bowl, combine all the marinade ingredients. Add the shrimp and marinate at room temperature for 30 minutes. Heat a frying pan over medium-high heat for 60 seconds. Add the olive oil and sauté the shrimp just until they turn pink, about 3 minutes; immediately transfer to a plate.

🌿 In a medium bowl, toss the greens with just enough lime-soy vinaigrette to lightly coat; reserve the leftover vinaigrette for another salad.

🌿 If using foie gras, heat a small frying pan over medium-high heat. Cook the foie gras until just browned around the edges, about 1 minute on each side. Transfer to a plate.

🌿 Arrange a mound of salad greens on each of 4 plates. Garnish each salad with shrimp, smoked salmon, prosciutto, quail eggs, and foie gras, if using. Sprinkle with coconut and serve at once. *Makes 4 servings*

*ABC brand sweet soy sauce is available at Asian markets.
**Fresh foie gras can be ordered from some butcher shops or from D'Artagnan at (800) 327-8246.

LIME-SOY VINAIGRETTE

1 tablespoon fresh lime juice

1 tablespoon fresh lemon juice

2 tablespoons soy sauce

$1/2$ tablespoon minced shallot

$1/2$ tablespoon grated peeled fresh
ginger

$1/2$ garlic clove, minced

$1/2$ cup extra-virgin olive oil

In a medium bowl, whisk all the ingredients together. *Makes about $3/4$ cup*

ROAST DUCK BREAST
WITH BLACK PEPPER CURRY

Serve this spectacular dish with sautéed baby bok choy and basmati rice.

SPICE MIX

2 tablespoons *each* curry powder,
cracked coriander seeds

1 tablespoon *each* ground cumin,
ground turmeric, garam masala*

1 tablespoon whole black peppercorns,
crushed

4 boneless duck breast halves, with skin

Salt for sprinkling

³/4 cup clarified butter (see Basics)

2 shallots, minced

¹/4 cup grated peeled fresh ginger

1 jalapeno chili, seeded and finely diced

3 garlic cloves, minced

¹/2 cup canned coconut milk

¹/2 cup duck or chicken stock (see
Basics) or canned low-fat chicken
broth

1 cup mixed dried fruit, such as raisins,
cranberries, and chopped apricots

Juice of 1 lime

¹/4 cup soy sauce

Fresh cilantro and cashews for garnish

To make the spice mix: In a spice grinder or mortar, combine the spice mix ingredients and grind to make a coarse powder. Set aside. Using a sharp knife, score a crisscross pattern in the skin of the duck breasts and sprinkle with salt. Heat a large frying pan over medium-low heat and cook the duck breasts, skin side down, for 8 minutes, or until golden brown. Pour off the fat. Turn the breasts over and cook on the second side for 3 minutes for medium rare. Transfer the duck to a cutting board, skin side down, and loosely cover with aluminum foil.

In a medium saucepan, heat the clarified butter over medium-high heat. Add spice mix, shallots, ginger, jalapeno, and garlic and sauté for 3 minutes. Stir in the coconut milk, stock or broth, dried fruits, lime juice, and soy sauce. Cook, stirring occasionally, for 10 to 15 minutes, or until slightly reduced and flavorful.

Cut the duck breasts into thin lengthwise slices. Fan the slices out on each of 4 warmed plates and spoon the black pepper curry sauce over. Garnish each plate with a cilantro sprig and cashews and serve immediately. *Makes 4 servings*

*Garam masala, a spice mixture that typically may include coriander, black pepper, cardamom, and cinnamon, can be found at Indian markets.

CRÈME BRÛLÉE

1 1/2 cups heavy cream
1/2 cup milk
1/4 vanilla bean, split lengthwise, or
   1/2 teaspoon vanilla extract

5 egg yolks
1/3 cup granulated sugar
8 teaspoons packed brown sugar

Preheat the oven to 275°F. In a small, heavy saucepan, combine the cream, milk, and vanilla bean, if using, and bring to a boil over medium heat. Remove from heat and set aside for 5 minutes to let the vanilla flavor infuse the milk. Remove the vanilla bean.

In a medium bowl, whisk the egg yolks and sugar together until pale. Whisk in one-third of the cream mixture. Gently stir in the remaining cream mixture and the vanilla extract, if using. Pour the custard into four 1/2-cup ramekins and set the ramekins in a large baking dish. Add hot water to come halfway up the sides of the ramekins. Bake in the oven for 1 hour, or until just set around the edges; the centers will still jiggle slightly. Let cool. Refrigerate for at least 2 hours or up to 24 hours.

Just before serving, preheat the broiler. Place 2 teaspoons of the brown sugar in a fine-mesh sieve and push the sugar through with the back of a spoon to evenly layer the top of a custard. Repeat for the remaining custards. Place the custards under the broiler about 2 inches from the heat source until the sugar is melted and crisp, 30 seconds to 1 minute. Or, use a blowtorch to caramelize the sugar. Let cool for a few minutes and serve. *Makes 4 servings*

AUGUST LOEFFLER *Bolton, Sept. 10th '64* 1864 The Adirondack Museum

GLENDORN, A LODGE IN THE COUNTRY
BRADFORD, PENNSYLVANIA

Built for a gregarious, multigenerational family during the 1930s, Glendorn is a 1,280-acre estate that offers luxurious accommodations, fine dining, and activities in the style of the great family "camps." The Dorn family loved recreation, learning, and rollicking good times, and they happily used the property as a summer and weekend home for over sixty years. Fortunately, in 1995 the family decided to open the estate to the public. Glendorn is an Orvis endorsed fly-fishing lodge, a member of the prestigious Relais & Chateaux organization, and was ranked by *Travel and Leisure* magazine as one of the 50 Most Romantic Places in the World. Both tranquil and spirited, Glendorn is a place to have fun!

MENU

*Three-Bean Soup
with Sausage and Cilantro*

*Pan-Seared Halibut Fillets on
Shrimp and Lobster Potato Cakes
with Corn Salsa and
Chili Butter Sauce*

*Warm Chocolate and
Coconut Croissant Pudding*

In the early 1900s, Clayton Glenville Dorn and his son Forest developed an innovative process that extracted oil from fields that were abandoned by the then-major oil companies of Pennsylvania. The process involved forcing water into the abandoned oil reservoirs, which floated out previously unobtainable oil. In 1916, C. G. Dorn and Forest Dorn founded Forest Oil Corporation to capitalize on the new process. As the Dorn family prospered and grew, C. G. Dorn, affectionately called Bondieu by family members in his later years, wanted to build a place for several generations of Dorns to enjoy. A philanthropist and humanitarian, Bondieu was also an avid outdoorsman. In 1928, he purchased an extraordinary parcel of land that included his favorite fishing camp on the banks of Fuller Brook, a fine trout stream. Over the years at Glendorn, the high-spirited Dorn family excelled at practical jokes, hired an Olympic swimmer to coach the family swimming team, and even built their own old-fashioned ice cream parlor for the many Dorn children.

Today Glendorn's social hub is the lodge, or Big House. It looks much as it did in the 1930s, with mostly original furnishings, family heirlooms, flickering candlelight from wrought-iron chandeliers, and lustrous first-growth redwood paneling. The house has

paintings by Dunton, Frost, and Gordon, which were given as thank-yous for visits in the early 1920s. The Big House includes the lodge's dining room, four elegant guest bedrooms, a recreation room, and the kitchen, with its glorious bread-baking ovens.

Twelve enchanting guest cabins are secluded in the woodlands that surround the lodge. Constructed by the Dorns in the 1930s and '40s for visiting family and friends, many of the cabins are reached by charming footbridges over rushing streams. These peaceful woody havens are perfect for couples and families and decorated in vintage fashion. Prominent guests have included Ella Fitzgerald, Art Buchwald, Louis Armstrong, and Victor Borge.

Glendorn guests are encouraged to take fly-fishing instruction from an Orvis pro, and there are miles of a private headwater stream and three small lakes stocked with brown, brook, and rainbow trout. Trap and skeet lessons are available, and many enjoy the seventeen miles of hiking trails in the shade of blue spruce, hemlock, and black cherry. The lodge supplies a trail guide to the local trees, shrubs, club mosses, and ferns. Cross-country skiing and snow-shoeing are popular in the winter, and in summer there's tennis, biking, and relaxing by the outdoor swimming pool. Special summer activities include raspberry and blackberry picking, after-dinner bonfires with Champagne and s'mores at Skipper Lake, movies on the lawn, and dinner served al fresco with music by a local jazz band.

The Great Hall in the Big House is a grand setting for candlelight dining. Guests gather for a sociable cocktail hour before seasonal four-course dinners. The meals are paired with well-chosen wine, and performances by a pianist set a romantic mood during dinner. Executive chef Diarmuid Murphy uses fresh local ingredients, and creative menus reflect his passion for cuisine that has no boundaries of style or country. After dinner, guests can shoot pool; play darts, chess, or cards; or try their hand at par puzzles. Glendorn is an easy place to make new friends, and conversations continue long after dinner. In the morning, breakfast is a major event that is served in courses. Chef Murphy created the following recipes and presented them to Menus and Music.

Managers Audrey and Dan Abrashoff and the extended Dorn family are dedicated to preserving the spirit of a vibrant American family. Visitors feel as though they are houseguests and return home with a trove of treasured experiences.

GLENDORN, A LODGE IN THE COUNTRY

A forest is not a mere collection of individual trees,

just as a city is not a mere collection of unrelated men and women,

or a Nation like ours merely a certain number

of independent racial groups. A forest, like a city, is a complex

community with a life of its own.

—Gifford Pinchot

THREE-BEAN SOUP
WITH SAUSAGE AND CILANTRO

At Glendorn, this hearty soup is made with venison sausage. Fresh pork sausage may be substituted. The soup can be prepared ahead of time and will keep for several days in the refrigerator. Reheat over low heat, adding more stock or broth if the soup is too thick.

$^1/_2$ cup *each* dried kidney beans, Great
   Northern beans, and black beans
1 fresh venison or pork sausage,
   about 6 ounces
1 tablespoon olive oil or canola oil
1 small onion, diced

3 garlic cloves, minced
8 cups chicken stock (see Basics) or
   canned low-salt chicken broth
Salt and freshly ground pepper to taste
$^1/_4$ cup minced fresh cilantro for
   garnish

Rinse and pick over the beans to remove any stones. Put the beans in a large bowl, add cold water to cover by 2 inches, and soak overnight; drain.

Using a fork, prick the sausage in several places. In a large saucepan over medium heat, heat the oil. Add the sausage and cook, turning several times, until well browned and firm, about 10 minutes. Transfer to a cutting board, let cool, and slice on the diagonal.

Pour off all but 1 tablespoon of the fat and sauté the onion for 3 minutes, or until translucent. Add the garlic and sauté for 2 minutes, or until fragrant. Add the beans, sausage, and stock or broth. Increase heat to high and bring to a boil, skimming off any foam that rises to the top. Reduce heat to low and simmer for 1 hour, or until the beans are soft and the soup has thickened. Season with salt and pepper. Ladle the soup into bowls, sprinkle with cilantro, and serve at once. *Makes 6 servings*

PAN-SEARED HALIBUT FILLETS ON SHRIMP AND LOBSTER POTATO CAKES WITH CORN SALSA AND CHILI BUTTER SAUCE

Delicately flavored halibut and potato cakes pair beautifully with this colorful salsa and lively sauce.

CORN SALSA

Kernels cut from 1 ear fresh corn

$1/2$ cup finely chopped pitted kalamata olives

$1/4$ cup finely diced roasted red bell pepper (see Basics)

1 tablespoon minced fresh chives

$1/4$ cup sweet chili sauce*

Salt and freshly ground pepper to taste

SHRIMP AND LOBSTER POTATO CAKES

2 Idaho potatoes, peeled and halved

4 ounces cooked shrimp, finely diced

8 ounces cooked lobster or lump crabmeat, picked over for shell, finely diced

6 green onions, white part only, thinly sliced

2 tablespoons minced fresh chives

Salt and freshly ground pepper to taste

2 tablespoons canola oil or clarified butter (see Basics)

CHILI BUTTER SAUCE

$1/4$ cup dry white wine

$1/4$ cup white wine vinegar

2 tablespoons heavy cream

$1/2$ cup (1 stick) cold unsalted butter, cut into pieces

1 tablespoon sriracha chili sauce*

Salt to taste

4 halibut fillets

Salt and freshly ground pepper to taste

2 tablespoons olive oil or canola oil

To make the corn salsa: In a medium bowl, combine all the ingredients. Cover with plastic wrap and set aside for at least 2 hours or up to 24 hours before serving.

To make the shrimp and lobster potato cakes: Cook the potatoes in boiling salted water for 20 minutes, or until very tender; drain. Transfer the potatoes to a medium bowl and use a large fork to mash them. Stir in the shrimp and lobster or crab. Add the green onions, chives, salt, and pepper and stir until thoroughly combined. Divide the potato mixture into 4 equal portions. Pack each portion into a 4-inch round metal ring to shape, or form them into 4-inch patties with your hands.

Heat a large frying pan over medium-high heat for 60 seconds. Add the oil or butter and fry the potato cakes for 5 minutes on each side, or until golden brown. Transfer to a baking sheet and set aside.

To make the chili butter sauce: In a medium saucepan, combine the wine and vinegar and cook over high heat until almost evaporated. Stir in the cream and bring to a boil. Remove from heat and whisk in the butter, sriracha chili sauce, and salt.

Sprinkle the halibut fillets with salt and pepper. Heat a large frying pan over medium-high heat for 60 seconds. Add the oil and sauté the halibut for 4 minutes on each side, or until golden brown on the outside and opaque throughout.

Place a shrimp and lobster potato cake in the center of each of 4 warmed plates and drizzle chili butter sauce around each cake. Top each potato cake with a halibut fillet and spoon a little corn salsa on top; serve immediately. *Makes 4 servings*

*Sweet chili sauce and sriracha, an Asian chili sauce, are available at Asian markets.

WARM CHOCOLATE AND
COCONUT CROISSANT PUDDING

A dish from chef Murphy's mother that is a popular dessert served at Glendorn.

4 croissants, halved lengthwise
6 ounces semisweet or bittersweet
   chocolate, chopped into small pieces,
   or 1 cup semisweet chocolate chips

$^1/_2$ cup sweetened shredded coconut
3 cups crème anglaise (recipe follows)
French vanilla ice cream for serving

Preheat the oven to 350°F. Arrange the bottom half of each croissant in an 8-inch square baking dish. Evenly sprinkle the croissants with the chopped chocolate or chocolate chips and half of the coconut. Top with the remaining croissant halves, placed upside-down, and sprinkle with the remaining coconut. Gently pour in the crème anglaise to evenly saturate the croissants.

Cover the baking dish with aluminum foil and bake in the preheated oven for 50 minutes, or until the custard is just set. Remove the foil and bake for 10 minutes, or until the top is golden brown and firm. Cut the pudding into 4 neat squares, then cut each square into 2 triangles. Place a triangle on each plate, top with a scoop of ice cream, and serve immediately. *Makes 8 servings*

CRÈME ANGLAISE

This light custard sauce can be used as a topping or be pooled under desserts.

6 egg yolks
$^3/_4$ cup sugar

2 cups milk
1 teaspoon vanilla extract

In a medium saucepan, whisk the egg yolks until blended. Gradually whisk in the sugar and continue whisking for 2 minutes, or until the mixture is pale and thick. In a small saucepan, heat the milk over medium-low heat until bubbles form around the edges of the pan. Gradually whisk the hot milk into the egg mixture. Return to the pan and cook, stirring constantly over medium heat, until the sauce thickens enough to coat the back of a spoon. Do not let the custard boil or the yolks will scramble. Remove from heat and stir in the vanilla. Let cool completely. Store, covered, in the refrigerator for up to 3 days. *Makes 3 cups*

WINSLOW HOMER *Casting, Number Two* 1894 National Gallery of Art

THE SWAG

WAYNESVILLE, NORTH CAROLINA

Visitors to the Swag come back year after year, returning to an atmosphere of relaxed comfort in the Great Smoky Mountains. A gentle dip in the mountaintop, known as a "swag" to local residents, gives this Mobil four-star-rated country inn its name. When owners Dan and Deener Matthews first bought the property to use as a family retreat, there was nothing on the land but trees and wildlife. Since then, the Matthews have created a rustic, elegant lodge with inviting cabins, tree-lined trails, and panoramic views.

MENU

Apple–Butternut Squash Soup

Almond-Crusted Beef Tenderloin
and Garlic Mashed Potatoes

Huckleberry Ice Cream

From late April through mid-November, guests can stay in cozy rooms or cabins built from rough-hewn logs and local stone and decorated with handmade quilts, woven rugs, and early-American antiques. The main lodge, designed by Dan Matthews, is made with century-old lumber gathered from five log structures in three different states.

Decks and balconies with handmade rocking chairs, and "hideaways" (outdoor hammocks and benches) scattered throughout the property are perfect for quiet conversation and for contemplation. A more active way to enjoy the Swag's 250 acres is the nature trail, a gentle three-mile loop with markers along the way identifying local flora and fauna. The trail crosses a charming swinging bridge near a waterwheel, passes the Swag's vegetable garden, and includes a visit to a rushing waterfall. For those who wish to venture farther afield, the property includes a private entrance to the trails of the Great Smoky Mountains National Park. At day's end, hikers look forward to a redwood sauna and an outdoor spa with a fifty-mile view.

Guests can learn more about the Smoky Mountains region at the Swag's special-events series. Throughout the season there are lectures on topics such as bird-watching, regional wildflowers, and "Black Bears and Other Unhuggables." Well-known artists, writers, and craftspeople offer workshops and evening talks. A favorite is the Art in Nature Workshop, which explores the design and construction of garden furnishings. Using local materials, participants build their own shelf, bench, or garden gate to take home.

At the Swag, breakfast typically includes cider-simmered oatmeal, Swag granola, fresh breads, and pancakes. Lunch is often a picnic, and dinner is a relaxed, sociable occasion. Award-winning contemporary American cuisine is served in a beautiful candlelit dining room. Guests are seated individually or family style at a long communal table, and there is singing around the player piano after dinner. Chef Matthew Frey created the following recipes and presented them to Menus and Music.

GREAT SMOKY MOUNTAINS NATIONAL PARK
NORTH CAROLINA/TENNESSEE

Great Smoky Mountains, America's most visited national park, is beloved for its gentle mountains, hidden waterfalls, and lush green forests of ancient trees. The park's name is a legacy of the Cherokee tribe who lived in the region and called this section of the Appalachian range Shaconage, or "Blue, Like Smoke."

In the late eighteenth century, the first settlers moved into the region, and in 1838, the U.S. government forced the entire Cherokee nation to leave their territories and march to Oklahoma. During this march, known as the "trail of tears," thousands of Cherokees died of illness, exhaustion, and grief. A small group of tribal members was allowed to stay in the southern Appalachian area, and their descendants now live on the Qualla Indian Reservation, on the southern boundary of the park.

The movement to create a national park in the southern Appalachians began in the late 1890s, but it wasn't until 1926 that Congress authorized the establishment of Great Smoky Mountains National Park. Major park supporters included local politicians, leading citizens, conservationists, and members of newly formed auto clubs, who saw the potential for beautiful drives along the scenic winding roads. Unlike most national parks west of the Mississippi, which were created from government-owned land, the Great Smokies had to be pieced together from over 6,000 tracts of private land. After a massive fundraising effort, the states of Tennessee and North Carolina bought more than 300,000 mountain acres. The land was transferred to the federal government, and years of hard work finally came to fruition in 1940 when President Franklin Roosevelt formally dedicated Great Smoky Mountains National Park.

Today the park consists of over 500,000 acres, almost 95 percent of which is forested. Favorite park activities include hiking, camping, fishing, and nature photography. Many tracts of old-growth forest give modern-day visitors a chance to experience the same untouched landscape that sheltered Native Americans and early Appalachian settlers. At the Mountain Farm Museum, there are historic farm buildings, including a log farmhouse, a barn, and a working blacksmith shop. At visitor centers located through-out the park, people can view exhibits about area history, purchase books and maps, and consult National Park Service rangers. The Smoky Mountain Field School, sponsored by Great Smoky Mountains National Park and the University of Tennessee, offers day and overnight hikes, as well as classes on navigation, photography, nature journaling, and the history, flora, and fauna of the region.

Since elevations in the Smokies range from 875 to 6,643 feet, the area is renowned for its biodiversity. There are five distinct kinds of forest, from hardwood forests on valley floors to spruce-fir forests in the mountains. Aside from visiting the Great Smokies, the only other way to see all five kinds of forest is to travel the eastern seaboard from Maine to Georgia! Great Smoky Mountains National Park was designated an International Biosphere Reserve in 1976, and in 1983 it became a World Heritage Site.

Visitors to Great Smoky Mountains National Park find comfort and inspiration in the lush beauty of its mountains and hospitable valleys.

APPLE–BUTTERNUT SQUASH SOUP

Chef Matthew Frey's full-flavored stock makes this soup memorable. Leftover stock can be used for another soup or for risotto.

3 small butternut squash, halved and seeded

4 tablespoons unsalted butter, melted, plus 1 tablespoon butter

3 Macintosh apples, peeled, cored, and quartered

4 leeks, white part only, 2 coarsely chopped and 2 thinly sliced

Grated zest of $1/2$ orange

$1/4$ teaspoon ground cinnamon

4 cups vegetable stock (recipe follows) or canned vegetable broth, plus more as needed

Salt and freshly ground pepper to taste

🍲 Preheat the oven to 450°F. Arrange 2 of the butternut squash, cut side up, in a 9-by-13-inch baking dish and generously brush the squash with 4 tablespoons of the melted butter. Fill each squash half with apple pieces. Cover the baking dish with aluminum foil and bake in the preheated oven for 1 hour, or until the squash are very tender when pierced with a fork. Let cool and scoop out the apples and the squash pulp. Transfer the squash and apples to a food processor and purée. Transfer the purée to a large bowl and set aside.

🍲 Peel the 1 remaining butternut squash and cut it into chunks. In a large stockpot, combine the squash, chopped leeks, orange zest, cinnamon, and vegetable stock or broth; bring to a boil. Reduce heat to low and simmer for 40 minutes, or until the squash is tender. Transfer the mixture to a food processor and purée until smooth.

🍲 In a large pot, combine the 2 purées and season with salt and pepper. Heat the soup over low heat. If it is too thick, add more vegetable stock.

🍲 In a small frying pan, melt the remaining 1 tablespoon butter over medium-high heat and sauté the sliced leeks for 5 minutes, or until golden brown. Ladle the soup into bowls and garnish each with a spoonful of sautéed leeks; serve hot. *Makes 10 to 12 servings*

VEGETABLE STOCK

3 carrots, peeled and coarsely chopped
Cloves from 1 head garlic
2 onions, quartered
2 parsnips, peeled and coarsely chopped
2 shallots
3 leeks, white part only, cut into
  large pieces

3 sprigs *each* fresh thyme, chervil,
  and parsley
1 bay leaf
2-inch piece fresh ginger, peeled
  and chopped
8 cups water

❧ In a large stockpot, combine all the ingredients and bring to a boil over high heat. Reduce heat to low and simmer for 1 to 2 hours. Remove from heat and strain through a fine-mesh sieve, pressing on the solids with the back of a large spoon. Cover and refrigerate for up to 3 days. To keep longer, bring the stock to a boil every 3 days, or freeze for up to 3 months. *Makes about 8 cups*

Nearly always there hovers over the high tops and around them a tenuous mist, a dreamy blue haze, like that of Indian summer, or deeper. Often it grows so dense as almost to shut out the distant view, as smoke does that has spread from a far-off forest fire. Then it is a 'great smoke' that covers all the outlying world; the rim of the earth is but a few miles away; beyond is mystery, enchantment.

—Horace Kephart

ALMOND-CRUSTED BEEF TENDERLOIN AND GARLIC MASHED POTATOES

A simple recipe that highlights the glorious flavor of beef tenderloin. Roast the garlic bulb for the garlic mashed potatoes alongside the beef.

1 1/2 pounds beef tenderloin, trimmed

2 eggs, lightly beaten

1/2 cup crushed almonds

Salt and freshly ground pepper to taste

Garlic Mashed Potatoes
  (recipe follows)

❧ Preheat the oven to 425°F. Coat the beef on all sides with the beaten eggs, then roll the meat in the almonds until evenly coated. Sprinkle all over with salt and pepper. Transfer the beef to a roasting pan and bake in the preheated oven for about 30 minutes, or until an instant-read thermometer inserted into the thickest part of the meat registers 122°F.

❧ Remove from the oven and let the beef rest for 10 minutes. Slice into very thin medallions and fan out the slices on each of 4 warmed plates. Add a mound of garlic mashed potatoes and serve immediately. *Makes 4 servings*

GARLIC MASHED POTATOES

4 red potatoes, peeled and quartered

1 garlic bulb, roasted (see Basics)

3 tablespoons finely shredded fresh
  basil (see Basics)

2 tablespoons unsalted butter

2 tablespoons olive oil

1/4 cup heavy cream or milk,
  plus more as needed

2 tablespoons freshly grated Parmesan
  cheese

Salt and freshly ground pepper to taste

In a medium saucepan, boil the potatoes in lightly salted water for 20 minutes, or until tender when pierced with a fork. Drain and transfer the potatoes to a large bowl. Add the roasted garlic, basil, butter, olive oil, and the 1/4 cup cream or milk and smash with a large fork, adding more cream or milk as needed to obtain the desired consistency. Fold in the Parmesan cheese and season with salt and pepper. *Makes 4 servings*

HUCKLEBERRY ICE CREAM

The acidity of white wine enlivens the flavor of fresh huckleberries or blueberries. Serve with your favorite cake or cookies.

1 1/2 cups fresh or frozen huckleberries
  or blueberries
1/4 cup dry white wine
1/4 cup water

1 cup sugar
2 cups heavy cream
1/4 teaspoon vanilla extract

In a medium nonaluminum saucepan, combine the huckleberries or blueberries, wine, and water. Bring to a boil, reduce heat, cover, and simmer for 10 minutes, or until the berries are soft.

Transfer the berry mixture to a food processor and purée. Strain the purée through a fine-mesh sieve and set aside.

In a medium nonaluminum saucepan, combine the sugar and 1 cup of the cream. Cook over medium heat, stirring until the sugar dissolves. Add the remaining 1 cup cream, the vanilla, and all but 3/4 cup of the huckleberry or blueberry purée. Transfer to a bowl and let cool. Cover and refrigerate until chilled, about 2 hours. Freeze in an ice cream maker according to the manufacturer's instructions. Serve topped with some of the reserved berry purée. *Makes about 1 quart*

After JOHN JAMES AUDUBON *Blue Heron* 1827–1838

CANOE BAY

CHETEK, WISCONSIN

Canoe Bay is known for luxurious lodging, fine cuisine, and a peaceful, secluded setting. Dan Dobrowolski, the lodge's current owner, spent many childhood hours exploring the property's forest and lakes while visiting his grandfather on a nearby farm. When the land came up for sale in the early 1990s, Dobrowolski and his wife Lisa decided to share their love for the Wisconsin woods by creating a romantic hideaway especially for couples. Located on a 280-acre forested estate, their highly civilized retreat is a member of the prestigious Relais & Chateaux organization.

MENU

Arugula, Smoked Salmon, and Toasted Hazelnut Salad

Roasted Pork Chops and Maple Whipped Sweet Potatoes with Pecan-Sage Sauce

Apple and Cranberry Cobbler with Vanilla Bean Ice Cream

When the Dobrowolskis purchased the property, they rebuilt all existing buildings using cedar wood and fieldstones. The design of the new buildings follows the principles of Wisconsin-born architect Frank Lloyd Wright, who believed buildings should be permanent works of art that harmonize with their environment. At Canoe Bay, guests can choose between a room in one of two main buildings or a private cottage. All accommodations have fireplaces, private decks, whirlpools for two, and handcrafted furniture.

For an especially luxurious visit, guests can choose to stay at one of Canoe Bay's two "signature" cottages. An architectural showcase, the Rattenbury cottage was designed by Frank Lloyd Wright protégé John Rattenbury. Soaring ceilings with clerestory windows, a clear-cedar interior, hardwood floors, and a massive stone fireplace all help to create an interior that blends perfectly with its surroundings. At the Lakeside Cottage, the ultimate in relaxation and pampering, guests enjoy a custom-built oversized bed, private Finnish sauna, giant picture windows, and a deck overlooking the lake.

Favorite activities at Canoe Bay include curling up by the fireside or relaxing with a favorite companion on the deck. Many visitors are tempted to spend hours in the Great

Room's extensive library of hardcover books and current magazines. The wooded property is crisscrossed with hiking trails, and boating, swimming, and catch-and-release fishing are possible on spring-fed lakes. Nearby, at the Chippewa Moraine Ice Age Center, visitors can learn about Wisconsin's glacial past. The Center is part of the Ice Age National Scenic Trail, a trail that showcases the dynamic glacial geology of Wisconsin.

Every morning at Canoe Bay, a breakfast of fresh-baked treats and organic fruits is quietly placed outside each guest's door. The perfect end to a day of rest or exploration is dinner in the lodge's elegant lakeside dining room. Chef Scott Johnson creates a different prix-fixe menu every night, using the finest naturally raised local foods. The restaurant's spectacular wine list has won *Wine Spectator* magazine's Award of Excellence, and guests can reserve a private table in the Canoe Bay wine cellar for special occasions. Chef Scott Johnson created the following recipes and presented them to Menus and Music.

The mission of an architect and of architecture is to help people

understand how to make life more beautiful . . .

—Frank Lloyd Wright

ARUGULA, SMOKED SALMON, AND TOASTED HAZELNUT SALAD

A superb salad with balanced tastes, colors, and textures.

Juice of $^1/_2$ lemon
Salt and freshly ground pepper to taste
$^1/_2$ cup extra-virgin olive oil
6 large handfuls baby arugula leaves
$^1/_2$ cup hazelnuts, toasted and skinned
   (see Basics)

1 cup Parmigiano-Reggiano cheese
   shavings
4 ounces thinly sliced smoked salmon,
   loosely rolled and cut into 1-inch-
   thick slices
Lemon zest strips for garnish (optional)

🍃 In a small bowl, whisk the lemon juice, salt, pepper, and olive oil together.
🍃 In a large bowl, toss the arugula with the vinaigrette until the leaves are lightly coated. Arrange a mound of salad on each of 4 plates and sprinkle with the toasted hazelnuts. Garnish each salad with cheese shavings, salmon slices, and optional lemon zest. *Makes 4 first-course servings or 2 main-course servings*

ROASTED PORK CHOPS AND MAPLE WHIPPED SWEET POTATOES WITH PECAN-SAGE SAUCE

This hearty main dish is delicious served with sugar snap peas and baby yellow squash.

PECAN-SAGE SAUCE

2 tablespoons olive oil
1 onion, finely chopped
2 tablespoons minced fresh sage leaves
1 sprig fresh thyme
1/2 cup dry red wine
2 cups beef stock (see Basics) or canned low-salt beef broth
1/4 cup pecans, toasted and chopped (see Basics)

MAPLE SWEET POTATOES

2 sweet potatoes, peeled and cut into 2-inch cubes
4 tablespoons unsalted butter at room temperature
2 tablespoons maple syrup
Salt and freshly ground pepper to taste
Milk as needed (optional)

4 bone-in center-cut pork chops
Salt and freshly ground pepper to taste
2 tablespoons olive oil

To make the pecan-sage sauce: In a medium saucepan over medium heat, heat the olive oil and sauté the onion for about 5 minutes, or until lightly browned. Stir in the sage, thyme, and wine, and cook until the wine is reduced by half. Add the stock or broth and cook for 30 minutes, or until the sauce is reduced by half. Strain through a fine-mesh sieve and stir in the pecans.

To make the sweet potatoes: In a medium saucepan, cook the sweet potatoes in salted boiling water for 20 to 30 minutes, or until tender when pierced with a fork. Drain and transfer to a food processor. Add the butter, maple syrup, salt, and pepper and purée. If the potatoes are too thick, add milk. Transfer to a bowl and keep warm.

To make the pork chops: Preheat the oven to 350°F. Season the pork chops with salt and pepper. In a large ovenproof frying pan over medium-high heat, heat the olive oil until almost smoking. Add the pork chops and brown for 1 minute on each side. Transfer the pan to the preheated oven and bake for 20 minutes, or until the meat is barely pink in the center.

To serve, spoon a mound of sweet potatoes in the center of each of 4 warmed plates. Spoon a pool of sauce next to the potatoes and top the sauce with a pork chop. Serve immediately. *Makes 4 servings*

APPLE AND CRANBERRY COBBLER
WITH VANILLA BEAN ICE CREAM

A delicious old-fashioned cobbler, baked in individual ramekins and served with home-made ice cream. The cobbler can also be cooked in one large baking dish.

Vanilla Bean Ice Cream
  (recipe follows)

TOPPING

2 cups all-purpose flour

1 teaspoon baking powder

1 teaspoon salt

1/2 cup sugar

1/2 cup (1 stick) cold unsalted butter,
  cut into small pieces

1/2 cup milk

FILLING

1 teaspoon ground cinnamon

1 teaspoon ground nutmeg

3 tart apples, such as Gravenstein,
  Pippin, or Granny Smith, peeled,
  cored, and cut into 2-inch cubes

1 cup fresh or frozen cranberries

1 cup sugar

1 teaspoon fresh lemon juice

To make the topping: In a medium bowl, combine the flour, baking powder, salt, and sugar. Stir to blend. Add the butter and rub it in with your fingers until the mixture resembles coarse crumbs. Pour in the milk and stir with a fork until just combined.

To make the filling: In a large bowl, combine all the ingredients and stir until well combined.

Preheat the oven to 350°F. Butter 4 individual ramekins or an 8-inch square baking dish. Divide the filling among the ramekins or pour into the baking dish and cover with the topping. Bake in the preheated oven for 40 to 50 minutes, or until the topping is golden brown. Remove and let cool for 10 minutes. Serve with a scoop of ice cream on top. *Makes 4 servings*

VANILLA BEAN ICE CREAM

1 cup milk

1 cup heavy cream

1/2 vanilla bean, split lengthwise, or

   1 teaspoon vanilla extract

4 egg yolks

1/2 cup sugar

In a medium saucepan, bring the milk, cream, and vanilla bean, if using, to a boil over medium heat; remove from heat.

In a medium bowl, whisk the egg yolks and sugar together until pale. Stir one-third of the hot cream mixture into the egg mixture. Return to the saucepan with the hot cream, reduce heat to low, and stir constantly until the mixture thickens enough to coat the back of a spoon. Strain through a fine-mesh sieve and stir in the vanilla extract, if using. Let cool, then refrigerate until chilled, at least 2 hours. Freeze in an ice cream maker according to the manufacturer's instructions. *Makes 1 pint*

CIBOLO CREEK RANCH
SHAFTER, TEXAS

I n true Texas fashion, the history of Cibolo Creek begins with a tall tale. Milton Faver, the story goes, was a young man trying to make his fortune in the Wild West. As settlers were wont to do in those days, he was involved in a duel, for reasons unknown. Fearing that he had killed his opponent, Faver fled to Texas. There, in the rugged Chinati and Cienega Mountains, the outlaw became a baron—one of the first and most successful cattle barons of the West. After Faver's death, his ranch and forts fell into disrepair. Almost a century later, Houston businessmen John Poindexter discovered the deserted ranch with its spring-fed lakes and Texas-sized views. Poindexter spent almost four years restoring Cibolo Creek to a working ranch and creating a renowned resort on the property. Using photographs, archives, and interviews with local residents, the old Faver-built forts were re-created as accurately as possible. Even the ranch's modern-day luxuries are carefully hidden, with electrical wiring covered by antique fixtures and bathroom doors concealed behind vintage furniture. Cibolo Creek has earned three listings in the National Register of Historic Places.

Guest accommodations are available at three separate sites on the property. The original main fort, El Fortin del Cibolo ("The Fort of the Buffalo"), is now ranch headquarters. Next door are twenty-two rooms in La Hacienda del Cibolo, a modern hacienda in the style of the old fort. El Fortin de la Cienega ("The Fort of the Marsh"), has five private rooms in the fort and seven more in an adjoining hacienda. The most intimate quarters at Cibolo Creek are in the guest cottage next to the beautifully austere El Fortin de la Morita ("The Fort of the Little Mulberry Tree"). This fort was left partially unfinished at the request of the Texas Historical Society. Each guest room at the ranch is individually decorated with Mexican and Spanish antiques, hand-stitched quilts, and vintage lamps. Luxurious bathrooms offer heated tile floors and pampering amenities.

Adventure seekers, history buffs, and art lovers can all satisfy their passions in this

---

MENU

Mixed Greens with Goat Cheese and Raspberry–Pink Grapefruit Vinaigrette

Venison Loin with Raspberry-Chipotle Sauce

Tres Leches Cake

remote area. There are miles of hiking and horseback riding trails on the ranch's thirty thousand acres, and a spring-fed lake is stocked for catch-and-release fishing. Traces of early settlers and miners can be seen in the neighboring ghost town of Shafter and at two private museums on the property. Cowboy singing, fireside lectures on local floral and fauna, and even authentic cattle drives (in season) can be arranged by request. At Big Bend National Park, about two hours away, there are opportunities for bird-watching, desert hiking, and float trips down the Rio Grande. After sundown, guests enjoy "Texas TV," otherwise known as lively conversation around a campfire, the only nighttime entertainment for cowboys in the days before television. Guests enjoy visiting nearby McDonald Observatory to learn about the stars visible in the Texas night sky and the Chinati Foundation, a world-famous contemporary art museum.

Since the nineteenth century, Cibolo Creek has been renowned for its gardens and orchards, and according to local legend Faver made an outstanding peach brandy with fruit from his own trees. Cibolo's cuisine still features fresh produce from the ranch. In addition, many dishes use Texas game and seafood, as well as tortillas and spices from across the border. Dining at Cibolo Creek is a social experience, usually enjoyed at long wooden tables in the dining room. Guests can also request a table by the swimming pool, on the veranda, or in the privacy of their own room. Chef Johnny D created the following recipes and presented them to Menus and Music.

CIBOLO CREEK RANCH

BIG BEND NATIONAL PARK

TEXAS

Big Bend National Park includes massive canyons, miles of the Rio Grande River, vast expanses of desert, and the entire Chisos Mountain Range. Situated on the border of Mexico along the Rio Grande, the park is named for a sharp turn, or "big bend," in the mighty river's course.

Signs of human habitation in the Big Bend region date back about 10,000 years. Since then, many Native American peoples—including members of the Chisos, Jumano, and Mescalero Apache tribes—have made their homes in what is now southwestern Texas. During the past 500 years, Texas has been a part of six different nations, including Spain, France, Mexico, the Republic of Texas, the Confederate States of America, and of course the United States. Big Bend National Park was authorized by Congress in 1935 and established in 1944. The park was designated as a United States Biosphere Reserve in 1976.

Today, Big Bend covers over 800,000 acres of Brewster County, one of the most sparsely populated areas of the United States. Remnants of the region's human history can be found in archeological sites throughout the park. In the Hot Springs Historic District, visitors can see rock art on limestone cliffs and imagine farms of corn, squash, and beans along the river's floodplain. The park's Castalon Historic District is situated close to the Mexican border. When two Castalon residents bought the town trading post in 1919, they named it La Harmonia Company Store with the hope of continued harmony between citizens

of Mexico and the United States. At the store, shoppers from both sides of the border could buy everything from barbed wire to ladies' dresses—including bridal wreaths and veils! Although Castalon's adobe homes and Texas ranger barracks have been abandoned, La Harmonia is now a National Park Service concession, selling snacks and groceries to park visitors.

Hiking and camping are a great way to experience Big Bend's unique ecosystems and desert wildlife. Along with coyote, black-tailed jackrabbits, javelina, mountain lions, and mule deer, the park is home to about 450 species of birds—more than any other American national park. Birders come from all over the United States to see species such as the Colima warbler, whose only North American home is Big Bend. To learn more about the park and its wildlife, visitors can attend ranger-led hikes, lectures, and slide shows. The Big Bend Natural History Association also offers seminars on topics such as "Wildflowers at Big Bend" and "Tracking in the Desert."

Float trips down the Rio Grande River give participants a unique view of canyon walls, riverside grasses, and animal life that ranges from peregrine falcons to wild horses. Visitors can bring their own boats, rent equipment, or hire a river guide. In 1978, the section of river that runs through Big Bend, plus an additional 127 miles downstream from the park, was designated the Rio Grande Wild and Scenic River. Because the Rio Grande serves as an international boundary, the park's jurisdiction extends only to the middle of the river's deepest channel.

Desert solitude and spectacular scenery reward travelers to Big Bend by day, and when night falls, the stars appear especially bright and numerous in this remote location. One enjoyable place to enjoy the night sky in the park is the hot springs located near Rio Grande Village.

Big Bend has an unusual and robust beauty. For many, the park's isolation offers an escape from the modern world into true American wilderness and a chance to experience the adventure of the frontier.

MIXED GREENS WITH GOAT CHEESE AND RASPBERRY–PINK GRAPEFRUIT VINAIGRETTE

Well balanced flavors and easy to make.

VINAIGRETTE
1 shallot, minced
Pinch of sugar
1 tablespoon raspberry vinegar
1 tablespoon pink grapefruit juice
Salt and freshly ground pepper to taste

6 tablespoons extra-virgin olive oil or
 canola oil

6 large handfuls baby salad greens
4 ounces fresh white goat cheese,
 crumbled (1 scant cup)

To make the vinaigrette: In a medium bowl, whisk all the ingredients together.

In a large bowl, toss the lettuce with the vinaigrette until the leaves are well coated. Arrange a mound of the salad on each of 4 plates and sprinkle with the goat cheese. *Makes 4 servings*

We simply need that wild country available to us, even if we never do

more than drive to its edge and look in. For it can be a means of reassuring

ourselves of our sanity as creatures, a part of the geography of hope.

—Wallace Stegner

VENISON LOIN WITH RASPBERRY-CHIPOTLE SAUCE

A tenderizing marinade and a spicy berry sauce complement venison's rich flavor. Venison is very lean and should not be overcooked, or it will become tough. Pork tenderloin can be substituted for the venison.

MARINADE

1 cup beef stock (see Basics) or canned low-salt beef broth

1 cup dry red wine

1 bay leaf or sprig fresh rosemary

2 garlic cloves, chopped

1 tablespoon cracked black peppercorns

2 pounds venison loin, silver skin removed

2 tablespoons olive oil

RASPBERRY-CHIPOTLE SAUCE

1 cup dry red wine

1 cup beef stock (see Basics) or canned low-salt beef broth

1 cup fresh or frozen raspberries

2 or 3 chipotle chilies in adobo,* chopped

1 tablespoon sugar, or to taste

2 tablespoons unsalted butter

Salt and freshly ground pepper to taste

In a bowl just large enough to hold the venison, combine all the marinade ingredients. Add the venison, turn to coat, and cover with plastic wrap. Refrigerate overnight, turning once or twice more.

Preheat the oven to 350°F. Remove the venison from the marinade (discard the marinade) and pat dry. Heat a large, ovenproof frying pan over medium-high heat for 60 seconds. Swirl in the olive oil and heat until almost smoking. Brown the meat on all sides, about 5 minutes total. Bake in the preheated oven for 15 to 20 minutes, or until an instant-read thermometer inserted in the thickest part of the meat registers 120°F for medium-rare. Remove from the oven, transfer to a plate, and cover loosely with aluminum foil; set aside.

(continued)

To make the sauce: In the same frying pan used to roast the venison, bring the red wine and beef stock or broth to a boil, stirring to scrape up any browned bits from the bottom of the pan. Stir in the raspberries, chipotles, and sugar and cook for 5 minutes, or until the liquid is reduced by half. Remove from heat and strain through a fine-mesh sieve, pressing on the solids with the back of a large spoon. Whisk in the butter until incorporated and season with salt and pepper. Slice the venison into medallions. Spoon a pool of sauce onto each of 4 warmed plates and arrange overlapping slices of meat over the sauce. Serve immediately. *Makes 4 servings*

*Chipotles in adobo are smoked, dried jalapeno chilies packed in a spicy sauce. They can be found in Latino markets and many supermarkets. Chipotles are medium hot and have a rich aroma and deep smoky flavor. Add 2 or 3 chilies depending on how spicy you want the sauce to be.

After JOHN JAMES AUDUBON *American Bittern* 1827–1838

CIBOLO CREEK RANCH

TRES LECHES CAKE

A dense, moist cake covered with satiny whipped cream, "three milks" cake has been popular for generations in Mexico and Central America. Serve with sliced peaches, strawberries, or pineapple, or a fruit salsa (see Basics).

CAKE

3/4 cup sugar

6 tablespoons butter at room temperature

4 eggs, separated

1 cup all-purpose flour

3/4 teaspoon baking powder

1/2 cup milk

1 teaspoon vanilla extract

1/2 teaspoon cream of tartar

TRES LECHES TOPPING

1 cup heavy cream

1 cup sweetened condensed milk

5 tablespoons evaporated milk

WHIPPED CREAM FROSTING

2 cups heavy cream

1/2 cup sugar

To make the cake: Preheat the oven to 350°F. Butter a 9-inch square baking dish. In a large bowl, use an electric mixer to beat the sugar and butter until pale and fluffy. Add the egg yolks and beat for 3 minutes, or until pale yellow.

In a small bowl, combine the flour and baking powder. Stir to blend. In another small bowl, combine the milk and vanilla. Alternately add the flour mixture and the milk mixture to the butter mixture by thirds and beat just until smooth.

In a large bowl, beat the egg whites and cream of tartar until soft peaks form. Fold the egg whites into the batter. Pour the batter into the prepared pan, smooth the top, and bake for 25 to 30 minutes, or until the cake is golden brown and a skewer inserted in the center comes out clean.

To add the topping: In a medium bowl, stir the 3 milks together until combined; do not beat. Unmold the cake while warm and use a skewer or fork to poke the top all over. Pour a little of the milk mixture evenly over the cake and let it soak in. Repeat until the cake will not absorb any more milk; you will have some milk mixture left over. Refrigerate the cake until chilled, at least 2 hours.

Just before serving, make the whipped cream frosting: In a deep bowl, beat the cream and sugar together until stiff peaks form. Frost the sides and top of the cake and serve. *Makes 1 cake*

HOME RANCH
CLARK, COLORADO

Set on the northern end of the beautiful Elk River Valley and near the outskirts of the Mount Zirkel Wilderness Area, Home Ranch carries on the tradition of Western hospitality at its best. The ranch is rated Four Stars by Mobil and is a twelve-year member of the prestigious Relais & Chateaux organization. Ken Jones is the builder and owner of this Rocky Mountain hideaway, which offers a gracious combination of Western warmth, creature comforts, and lively outdoor activity.

The ranch has six rooms in the main lodge, and eight comfortable cabins surrounded by aspens and decorated with Western antiques, original artwork, cozy down comforters, and wood-burning stoves. The hot tub on each private cabin porch is especially welcome after a day of riding, hiking, or skiing. Lodge rooms in the main building are close to the dining and great rooms.

Guests at Home Ranch enjoy outstanding horsemanship programs for adults and children suitable for all levels of ability. A variety of rides are offered each day, including trail rides, lunch rides, all-day rides, and lessons. Cattle-working classes and special horse clinics are offered from May to the end of September. For those who relish summer afternoons of quiet stillness, fly-fishing is available just steps from the lodge in a stocked trout pond. There is also fishing on two miles of pristine, private water along the Elk River, which is best for rainbow, cutthroat, and brown trout after mid-July. The Home Ranch supplies top-of-the-line fly rods and reels as well as waders. Guests can hike with local guides on scenic hiking trails through the Routt National Forest and the Mount Zirkel Wilderness Area, with alpine lakes that are perfect destinations for all-day hikes. Back at the ranch there is a lap pool and sauna, and evening activities that include cookout hayrides, barn dances, and songs around the campfire.

MENU

Quesadillas with Brie Cheese, Mango, and Chilies

Grilled Beef Tenderloin with Ranch Tomato Sauce

Caramelized Corn

Grilled Vegetables

Chocolate Bread Pudding with Bourbon Custard Sauce

In winter, Home Ranch changes from dude ranch to snowy paradise. There is cross-country skiing on groomed trails through the Elk River Valley, snow-shoeing, and sleigh rides. Complimentary equipment is available for guest use, and for the more adventurous, there are off-ranch excursions led by local guides. Downhill skiing and shopping are available at the Steamboat ski area, just eighteen miles away.

Guests talk about the food served at Home Ranch long after they leave. Chef Clyde Nelson's gourmet Western fare is served with continental flair in a down-home atmosphere. During the summer there are campfire cookouts and dinners in the barn with a music show featuring Cowboy Ken and the Ranch Hand Band. During quieter winter evenings, guests can leave the world behind and enjoy leisurely formal dinners after days of winter activity. Chef Clyde Nelson created the following recipes and presented them to Menus and Music.

The Home Ranch offers a step back in time and a taste of life on an authentic ranch. Guests return home with a spring in their step and treasured memories of the West.

QUESADILLAS WITH
BRIE CHEESE, MANGO, AND CHILIES

A delicious, festive appetizer.

1 onion, thinly sliced

1 poblano chili,* roasted and chopped
(see Basics)

1 red bell pepper, roasted and chopped
(see Basics)

2 tablespoons unsalted butter, melted

2 tablespoons olive oil

1 mango, peeled, pitted, and diced

2 tablespoons chopped fresh cilantro

8 ounces chilled Brie cheese, rind
removed, cut into $1/4$-inch-thick slices

Salt and freshly ground pepper to taste

Four 8-inch flour tortillas

In a small saucepan, bring $1/2$ cup water to a boil. Add the onion, cover the pan, and remove from heat. Let stand for 10 minutes, or until the onion is wilted; drain.

In a small bowl, combine the poblano chili, bell pepper, and onion. (This mixture can be prepared 1 day ahead. Cover with plastic wrap and refrigerate.)

Prepare a fire in a charcoal grill or preheat the broiler.

In a small bowl, combine the melted butter and olive oil. Stir the mango and cilantro into the poblano chili mixture.

Place one-fourth of the cheese slices on half of each tortilla. Top with one-fourth of the chili mixture. Season with salt and pepper. Fold over half of each tortilla to enclose the filling. Brush each quesadilla on both sides with the butter mixture.

Place the quesadillas on the grill or under the broiler. Cook for 30 seconds, then turn 90 degrees and cook 30 seconds longer. Turn the tortillas over and cook until the cheese begins to melt, about 30 seconds. Transfer to a cutting board and cut each quesadilla into 3 pieces. Arrange the quesadillas on a platter and serve at once. *Makes 4 to 6 servings*

*A fresh dark-green chili, sometimes called a pasilla in California, available at some grocery stores and Latin American markets.

GRILLED BEEF TENDERLOIN
WITH RANCH TOMATO SAUCE

This dish is traditionally served at the Home Ranch Saturday-evening cookout. Guests gather to enjoy a farewell dinner and an evening of sentimental songs around the campfire.

DRY RUB

3 tablespoons salt

3 tablespoons freshly cracked pepper

2 tablespoons minced garlic

1 tablespoon sweet Hungarian paprika

2 teaspoons crumbled bay leaf

1 1/2 teaspoons cayenne pepper

1 1/2 teaspoons dry mustard

1/4 cup chopped fresh parsley, squeezed dry

1 beef tenderloin, about 4 pounds, trimmed

BBQ MOPPING SAUCE

1 cup beef stock (see Basics) or canned low-salt beef stock

1/4 cup dry red wine

1/4 cup Worcestershire sauce

2 tablespoons olive oil

2 serrano chilies, crushed

2 garlic cloves, crushed

3 tablespoons bottled barbecue sauce

Salt and freshly ground pepper to taste

RANCH TOMATO SAUCE

2 tablespoons olive oil

1 red onion, chopped

2 garlic cloves, minced

2 poblano chilies, seeded, deribbed, and chopped

5 ripe tomatoes, peeled, seeded, and diced

1 teaspoon minced fresh oregano

1 teaspoon minced fresh basil

1 cup tomato sauce

1 tablespoon red wine vinegar

Salt and freshly ground pepper to taste

2 tablespoons unsalted butter

In a small bowl, combine all the ingredients for the dry rub. Rub your hands with olive oil and rub the dry rub into the tenderloin, coating it well. Let stand for 20 minutes.

In a medium bowl, combine all the ingredients for the mopping sauce. Stir to blend.

To make the ranch tomato sauce: In a medium saucepan over medium heat, heat the olive oil and sauté the onion for 3 minutes. Add the garlic and sauté for 2 minutes, or until fragrant. Stir in the chilies, tomatoes, oregano, basil, tomato sauce, and vinegar. Reduce heat to medium-low and cook for 10 to 15 minutes, or until the sauce thickens. Season with salt and pepper. Set aside and keep warm.

Prepare a fire in a charcoal grill. Grill the tenderloin for 5 minutes. Brush the meat with the mopping sauce. Turn the meat over and grill for 5 minutes. Repeat twice to sear all 4 sides of the meat. Turn the meat over to the first side, turning it 90 degrees to make crisscross grill marks. Cook about 10 minutes longer, a total of 30 minutes, or until an instant-read thermometer inserted in the center of the meat registers 120° to 125°F for rare and 130°F for medium rare.

Move the meat to a cooler part of the grill, cover it loosely with aluminum foil, and let rest for 10 to 15 minutes. Slice the tenderloin. Whisk the butter into the warm ranch tomato sauce and serve the sliced meat with the sauce. *Makes 8 to 10 servings*

CARAMELIZED CORN

4 ears of corn, husked
1/2 tablespoon corn oil or olive oil

Salt and freshly ground pepper to taste
Balsamic vinegar to taste

Using a sharp knife, cut the corn kernels from the cobs. In a heavy frying pan over medium-high heat, heat the corn oil or olive oil and add the corn kernels. Cook until the corn begins to brown and some kernels pop. Transfer to a bowl and toss the corn with the salt, pepper, and balsamic vinegar. *Makes 4 cups*

GRILLED VEGETABLES

The basil marinade also makes a great dipping oil for your favorite bread.

BASIL MARINADE

2 cups extra-virgin olive oil

2 tablespoons chopped shallot

1 tablespoon chopped garlic

2 tablespoons chopped fresh basil

2 tablespoons chopped fresh parsley

4 dried sage leaves

2 tablespoons fresh lemon juice

1 tablespoon grated Parmesan cheese

1 tablespoon pine nuts

2 teaspoons *each* salt and freshly
  ground pepper

2 Japanese eggplants, halved lengthwise

2 zucchini, halved lengthwise

2 red bell peppers, seeded, deribbed,
  and cut into thirds

2 yellow bell peppers, seeded,
  deribbed, and cut into thirds

1 small jicama, peeled and cut into
  $1/4$-inch-thick crosswise slices

1 bunch green onions

8 stalks asparagus, trimmed

To make the basil marinade: In a food processor, combine all the ingredients and purée.

In a large bowl, combine the eggplants, zucchini, bell pepper, jicama, green onions, and asparagus. Pour over enough marinade to lightly coat the vegetables and toss well. Let sit at room temperature for 1 hour before grilling. Reserve the remaining marinade to pour over the grilled vegetables.

Prepare a fire in a charcoal grill or preheat the broiler. Grill the vegetables over hot coals on both sides to make grill marks, then cook over indirect heat at the side of the grill until tender. Or, broil the vegetables under the preheated broiler until they are lightly charred, then bake in a preheated 400°F oven until tender. Arrange the vegetables on a serving platter and pour over some of the reserved marinade. *Makes 8 servings*

CHOCOLATE BREAD PUDDING
WITH BOURBON CUSTARD SAUCE

A luscious pudding that is good for company, because it can be prepared ahead and sliced just before serving.

4 ounces semisweet chocolate,
  chopped
1 1/2 cups heavy cream or
  half-and-half
1 1/2 cups milk
1/8 teaspoon salt
6 egg yolks

1/2 cup sugar
1/2 teaspoon vanilla extract
12 slices (12 ounces) white bread,
  crusts removed
6 tablespoons unsalted butter, melted
Bourbon Custard Sauce
  (see Basics)

❧ Preheat the oven to 325°F. In a medium saucepan, combine the chocolate, heavy cream or half-and-half, milk, and salt. Cook over low heat, stirring frequently, until the chocolate melts. Remove from heat.

❧ In a medium bowl, whisk the egg yolks, sugar, and vanilla together. Gradually whisk in the hot chocolate mixture. Set aside.

❧ Slice the bread into 1/2-inch-thick slices. Cut each slice lengthwise into 3 to 4 strips.

❧ Butter a 7-by-11-inch baking dish. Brush both sides of the sliced bread with melted butter and arrange the strips in neat rows in the baking dish. Pour the chocolate custard over the bread and set aside for least 30 minutes, pushing the bread down occasionally so it will absorb the custard.

❧ Place the pudding dish in a larger baking dish and fill the larger dish with hot water to come halfway up the sides of the pudding. Bake in the preheated oven for 30 minutes, or until a knife inserted in the center comes out clean. Let cool for at least 15 minutes. Cut the warm pudding into squares and serve with bourbon custard sauce. *Makes 8 to 12 servings*

THE LODGE AT VAIL
VAIL, COLORADO

Located in one of the most popular ski resorts in North America, the Lodge at Vail combines Old World elegance with the warmth of traditional Western hospitality. Guests enjoy the lodge's relaxed elegance, impeccable service, and highly desirable ski-in/ski-out location.

The town of Vail has grown around a ski resort that was founded by two passionate skiers, Peter Seibert and Earl Eaton. In 1957, Siebert, who was familiar with the Colorado Rocky Mountains, led Eaton on a seven-hour hike to a summit about one hundred miles from Denver. The two men agreed that they had found the perfect location for a new American skiing community. They bought a 500 acre ranch at the foot of the mountain and named it after Charles Vail, the engineer in charge of building a mountain pass through the area during the 1930s. The National Forest Service had jurisdiction over the mountainside and stipulated that the new ski area had to include at least one lodge with rooms for thirty guests. A rustic chalet-style lodge was opened to satisfy this requirement. Since then, the Lodge at Vail has grown to include 123 hotel rooms and condominiums, as well as 44 chalet-style condominium suites. All accommodations are individually decorated, and many have fireplaces, balconies, and breathtaking views of Vail Mountain.

Vail's more than 5,000 acres of terrain for skiing and snowboarding include gentle beginner's runs as well as moguls and bowls for experts. For a day away from the slopes, the town of Vail is a perennial favorite, with pedestrian-only streets, Tyrolean-style architecture, and inviting stores and galleries. The lodge can help guests plan activities, such as snowshoeing through White River National Forest, ice skating, and romantic rides in a horse-drawn sleigh. When the snow has melted, sport enthusiasts enjoy golfing, hiking, fishing, rafting, mountain biking, and hot-air ballooning. The Betty Ford Alpine Gardens,

MENU

Cream of Parsnip
and Salsify Soup with
Toasted Almonds and
Cinnamon Walnut Oil

Macadamia Nut–Crusted
Ahi Tuna with
Crab Risotto and Leek Sauce

Orange-Scented Chocolate Tart
with Chocolate-Tea Sorbet

. . . I started dreaming about finding a new ski area. I started climbing mountains,

looking and dreaming. That's when I started looking at Vail Mountain . . .

—Earl Eaton

another delightful warm weather destination, are just a short walk from the lodge. Here, in the world's highest botanic garden, visitors can learn about native plant life and stroll among beautiful alpine wildflowers. For music lovers, the Vail Music Festival stages open-air concerts performed by the New York Philharmonic and Rochester Philharmonic Orchestras.

An elegant meal at the Wildflower, the Lodge at Vail's Mobil four-star restaurant, is the perfect end to a day of sports and sightseeing. The Wildflower serves creative American cuisine prepared with finest produce, seafood, and meats. Chef Thomas Newsted changes the menu regularly to take advantage of seasonal fruits and vegetables, including herbs grown in the Vail garden. The restaurant's extensive wine list has earned the Wine Spectator's Best of Award of Excellence, and a special wine- and food-tasting menu can be arranged with the sommelier's assistance. In the dining room, hand-painted murals and giant baskets with flowers create a delightful atmosphere. During summer months, guests can enjoy alfresco dining on the terrace, surrounded by colorful wildflowers. Chef Thomas Newsted created the following recipes for Menus and Music.

CREAM OF PARSNIP AND SALSIFY SOUP WITH TOASTED ALMONDS AND CINNAMON WALNUT OIL

Subtle flavors combine in this luxurious, warming soup.

1 tablespoon unsalted butter

1/2 small onion, chopped

1 apple, peeled, cored, and chopped

1 celery stalk, chopped

1/4 cup Nocello (walnut liqueur) or Frangelico (hazelnut liqueur)

2 pounds parsnips, peeled and chopped

8 ounces salsify*, peeled and chopped

1 bay leaf

5 white peppercorns

4 cups chicken stock (see Basics) or canned low-salt chicken broth

2 cups heavy cream or half-and-half

Salt and ground white pepper to taste

GARNISHES

2 tablespoons sliced almonds

2 teaspoons ground cinnamon

2 tablespoons walnut oil

❧ In a large saucepan, melt the butter over medium-low heat and sauté the onion, parsnips, apple, and celery for 5 minutes. Add the walnut or hazelnut liqueur and cook until most of the liqueur evaporates. Add the salsify, bay leaf, peppercorns, and stock or broth and simmer for 15 minutes, or until reduced by one-third. Stir in the cream or half-and-half and simmer for 20 to 25 minutes, or until the vegetables are very tender.

❧ In a dry sauté pan over medium-high heat, toast the sliced almonds until golden brown; set aside.

❧ In a small frying pan over medium-high heat, toast the cinnamon until fragrant. Remove from heat and whisk in the walnut oil; transfer to a small bowl.

❧ In a blender or food processor, purée the soup, in batches if necessary. Strain through a fine-mesh sieve back into the saucepan and season the soup with salt and pepper. Ladle into 4 bowls and float the toasted sliced almonds on the soup. Use a teaspoon to drizzle the cinnamon-walnut oil around the almonds and serve hot. *Makes 4 servings*

* Salsify, also called oyster plant, is a root vegetable with a delicate oysterlike flavor. It is available in some grocery stores and at specialty produce markets.

MACADAMIA NUT–CRUSTED AHI TUNA
WITH CRAB RISOTTO AND LEEK SAUCE

Chef Tom Newsted finishes this dish with drizzles of bottled fig sauce that has been reduced to a syrup.

MACADAMIA NUT CRUST

1/4 cup ground macadamia nuts

1/4 cup all-purpose flour

LEEK SAUCE

2 tablespoons olive oil

6 leeks, white part only, rinsed and
  coarsely chopped

2 celery stalks, coarsely chopped

1/2 cup dry white vermouth

2 cups chicken stock (see Basics) or
  canned low-salt chicken broth

2 cups fish stock (see Basics) or
  canned low-salt chicken broth

1 bay leaf

6 white peppercorns

12 parsley stems

Salt and freshly ground white pepper
  to taste

Four 4-ounce ahi tuna loins, each cut
  into a rectangle

Salt and ground white pepper to taste

2 tablespoons clarified butter
  (see Basics)

Crab Risotto (recipe follows)

1/2 tablespoon unsalted butter

🐟 To make the macadamia nut crust: In a small bowl, combine the ingredients and stir to blend. Set aside.

🐟 To make the leek sauce: In a medium saucepan over medium heat, heat the olive oil and sauté the leeks and celery for 3 minutes. Stir in the vermouth and cook until almost evaporated. Pour in the chicken stock or broth and fish stock or chicken broth. Bring to a simmer and stir in the bay leaf, white peppercorns, and parsley. Simmer for 30 minutes, or until reduced by one-third. In a blender or food processor, purée until smooth. Strain the sauce through a fine-mesh sieve. Add salt and pepper and set aside.

🐟 Preheat the oven to 350°F. Season the tuna with salt and pepper on all sides. Spread the macadamia nut crust in a pie plate. Roll each tuna loin in the macadamia nut crust to coat the 4 long sides.

(continued)

In a large, heavy frying pan over medium-high heat, heat the clarified butter until it starts to pull away from the sides of the pan. Add the tuna on one of its crusted sides and cook for 45 seconds, or until golden brown; turn and repeat for all crusted sides. Turn each tuna rectangle to one of the uncrusted sides and bake in the preheated oven for 2 minutes. Remove from the oven, turn each tuna rectangle to the other side without crust, and bake for 1 minute.

To serve, reheat the risotto over low heat. Spoon it into a 5-inch ring mold in the center of a plate; remove the mold. Repeat with 3 other plates. Bring the leek sauce to a boil, remove from heat, and swirl in the $^1/_2$ tablespoon butter. Spoon the leek sauce around the risotto. Using a sharp knife, cut the tuna into thin diagonal slices and place slightly overlapping slices on top of each risotto cake; serve at once. *Makes 4 servings*

CRAB RISOTTO

2 tablespoons olive oil
$^1/_2$ cup finely diced onion
2 garlic cloves, minced
2 cups Arborio rice
2 cups dry white wine
8 cups vegetable stock (see Basics) or canned low-salt vegetable broth, heated

$^1/_4$ cup finely diced yellow bell pepper
8 ounces fresh lump crabmeat, picked over for shell
4 tablespoon unsalted butter
4 tablespoons grated Parmesan cheese
Salt and freshly ground pepper to taste
$^1/_4$ cup chopped fresh chives

In large frying pan over medium heat, heat the olive oil and sauté the onion for 3 minutes. Add the garlic and sauté for 1 minute, or until fragrant. Add the rice and stir until opaque, about 2 minutes. Add the wine and stir constantly until the liquid is absorbed. Add $^1/_2$ cup of the stock or broth and stir constantly until absorbed. Repeat, adding the remaining stock or broth $^1/_2$ cup at a time until the rice is tender but firm, about 20 minutes. Add the bell pepper, crab, and butter and stir for 1 minute. Stir in the Parmesan cheese, salt, pepper, and chives. Set aside and let cool. *Makes 4 servings*

ORANGE-SCENTED CHOCOLATE TART
WITH CHOCOLATE-TEA SORBET

Delicious served with the same black tea used to make the chocolate-tea sorbet.

PASTRY

1 cup all-purpose flour

1 tablespoon powdered sugar

1 tablespoon unsweetened cocoa
powder

7 tablespoons cold unsalted butter, cut
into small pieces

1 egg yolk

2 tablespoons cold water

FILLING

10 ounces bittersweet chocolate,
chopped

7 tablespoons unsalted butter

$1/3$ cup heavy cream

$1/3$ cup sugar

4 eggs

1 egg yolk

2 tablespoons Grand Marnier

Chocolate-Tea Sorbet (recipe follows)

To make the pastry shell: Preheat the oven to 350°F. In a food processor, add
the flour, powdered sugar, cocoa, and butter. Process until the mixture resembles
coarse crumbs, about 15 seconds. With the machine running, add the egg yolk
and water and process until the dough just begins to form a ball. Flatten the
dough into a disk, cover with plastic wrap, and refrigerate for at least 30 minutes.

Preheat the oven to 375°F. On a lightly floured surface, roll the dough out
to a 10-inch round. Fit into a 9-inch fluted tart pan, roll a rolling pin over the
rim to trim the edges, and refrigerate for 30 minutes. Prick the pastry with a fork.
Line the shell with aluminum foil and fill with dried beans or pastry weights.
Bake in the preheated oven for 15 minutes. Remove aluminum foil and the
beans or weights. Set aside to cool.

(continued)

To make the filling: In a double boiler over simmering water, melt the chocolate and butter with the cream; remove from heat.

In a medium metal bowl, whisk the eggs and the egg yolk together with the sugar until fluffy. Set the bowl over barely simmering water and whisk constantly until thickened, about 10 minutes. Be careful not to let the egg mixture boil, or it will curdle. Remove from heat and fold in the chocolate mixture and Grand Marnier. Pour the filling into the tart shell and shake the pan lightly to level the filling. Bake in the preheated oven for 10 to 15 minutes, or until set and lightly firm. Let cool, cover with plastic wrap, and refrigerate until chilled. Serve wedges of pie topped with chocolate-tea sorbet. *Makes one 9-inch pie*

CHOCOLATE-TEA SORBET

2 cups water

$^1/_2$ cup unsweetened cocoa powder

2 tablespoons sugar

4 ounces bittersweet chocolate, chopped

1 tablespoon corn syrup

Grated zest of 2 oranges

$^1/_4$ cup loose-leaf black tea such as Earl Grey or Darjeeling

In a medium, heavy saucepan, combine all the ingredients and bring to a boil over medium-high heat. Remove from heat and let stand for 1 hour. Strain the liquid through a fine-mesh sieve into a medium bowl and refrigerate until chilled, at least 2 hours. Transfer to an ice cream maker and freeze according to the manufacturer's instructions. *Makes 1 pint*

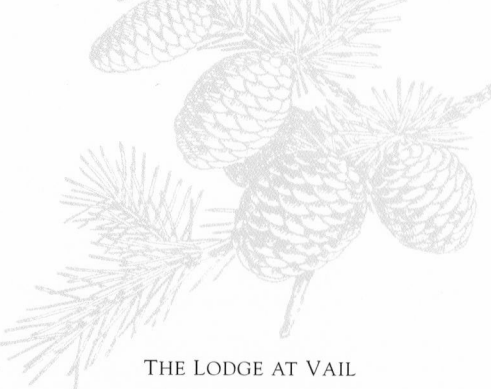

LAKE YELLOWSTONE HOTEL
YELLOWSTONE NATIONAL PARK

Long known as a meeting place and camping spot by Indians, trappers, and mountain men, the Lake Hotel's breathtaking site overlooks one of the world's largest alpine lakes. A vision of neoclassical grandeur with a marvelously restored 1920s-style interior, Yellowstone's oldest hotel is one of the most delightful summer hotels in the world.

Built in 1889, the Lake Hotel was a Northern Pacific Railroad building along Yellowstone Park's Grand Loop Road. At that time, the railroad held a near monopoly on travel to Yellowstone, and the hotel was built in order to capitalize on the park's amazing potential as a tourist attraction.

Between the early 1900s and the late 1920s, architect Robert Reamer transformed the originally plain clapboard building into a stylish resort hotel. Mr. Reamer envisioned a grand building where park visitors could enjoy elegance while surrounded by wilderness. His designs and remodels added stately Ionic columns, extended gables, and false balconies. Following World War I, a massive porte cochere was added to the hotel entrance that enabled touring cars and buses to drop off passengers and baggage in all kinds of weather. During the 1920s, Reamer extensively remodeled the hotel lobby, creating its renowned fireplace and fanciful drinking fountain and adding a large lounge that extended toward Yellowstone Lake. In this lounge, visitors relaxed in style and enjoyed performances on the hotel's mahogany grand piano and views of the snow-capped Abrasoka range across the lake.

During the Great Depression, people had to cut back traveling and vacationing, and in 1932 the Lake Hotel was closed for a few years. Although the hotel reopened in 1937, only necessary maintenance and refurbishing was done during the years before World War II. During the war, the hotel closed again, and by the mid-1950s some people even considered tearing down the entire building. Instead, there was a haphazard fifties-style remodeling,

MENU

White Bean Purée,
Baked Shiitake Mushrooms, and
Roasted Red Peppers

Duck Breast Roulade
with Cognac Sauce, Polenta,
and Haricots Verts

French Crumb Cake
with Huckleberry Sauce

and profits continued to decline. In 1959, a strong earthquake rattled Yellowstone, and for a while visitors avoided the park altogether.

In 1972, Yellowstone Park celebrated its one-hundredth birthday, and centennial preparations included rerouting the Grand Loop to bypass the traditional Lake Hotel front-door approach. Instead, tour buses brought visitors to a makeshift back-door entrance that gave way to a disappointingly threadbare interior. Fortunately, in 1979 an ambitious program was started to restore the Lake Hotel's reputation for quality. New management invested profits in repairs, maintenance, and capital improvements. Extensive lobby, lounge, and dining room renovations took place in 1985, and original hotel furnishings were taken out

of storage, where they had been since 1929. By the time the hotel celebrated its centennial in 1991, it had regained the reputation it was known for during its 1920s glory years, when dining room "crowds were so great as to require two or three sittings."

Today, Lake Hotel guests relax in classic, casual elegance. Entering past stately Ionic columns, they can admire an original 1937 White Motor Company Model 706 parked in the porte cochere. This vintage touring bus is available for photo safaris and sunset tours with an entertaining and knowledgeable guide. Other activities include guided fishing trips, scenic cruises on Yellowstone Lake, and wildlife-viewing excursions to Lamar Valley.

The Lake Hotel's pastel interior color scheme and polished hardwood floors create an airy, clean feel, and wicker furniture and decorative accents establish a classic 1920s ambiance. In the Sun Room, guests can enjoy drinks while listening to the Lake String Quartet or a pianist. In the evening, the casually elegant dining room is a perfect setting for delightfully extravagant dining. Executive chef Bo Cleveland created the following recipes for Menus and Music.

YELLOWSTONE NATIONAL PARK

IDAHO/MONTANA/WYOMING

In 1872, tens of millions of bison roamed the West in a still-intact wilderness. In that year, Congress set aside a piece of wilderness that was so overwhelmingly magnificent that it deserved designation as the country's, as well as the world's, first national park. Yellowstone is where bison, the symbol of the National Park Service, were rescued from the brink of extinction in North America. A thermal wonderland, the park holds two-thirds of the world's geysers and is an International Biosphere Reserve and a World Heritage Site. Yellowstone is a dynamic wild ecosystem, one of only a handful left in the world.

A series of volcanic eruptions formed the geology of Yellowstone between two million and 600,000 years ago. The volcanic activity that caused those eruptions still generates enough energy to create the park's amazing display of hot springs, geysers, mudpots, and fumaroles. Since Yellowstone has the largest concentration of free-roaming wildlife in the lower forty-eight states, visitors come here to see herds of bison and elk, grizzlies, wolves, Yellowstone cutthroat trout, bald eagles, and great gray owls, among many other species. There are excellent day and evening programs by National Park Service rangers, more than 1,200 miles of marked hiking trails, guided cross-country ski and snowshoeing tours, horseback riding trips, fishing, and boating. For those who want to explore the park with informative and entertaining naturalists and stay in comfort at night, "Lodging and Learning" programs are available through the Yellowstone Association and in partnership with Xanterra Parks & Resorts.

A figure-eight-shaped road system loops more than one hundred miles through Yellowstone's five distinct regions and gives travelers a glimpse of many of the park's major attractions. In Geyser Country, the most-visited Yellowstone area, Old Faithful spouts off, sending thousands of gallons of water 135 feet into the sky approximately every seventy-four minutes. In Canyon Country, the Yellowstone River roars through the cliffs of the vast Grand Canyon of the Yellowstone, which includes the thunderous Lower Falls, twice as high as Niagara Falls. In Roosevelt Country, there are stagecoach rides and Western cookouts that recapture the Old West, as well as volcanic pinnacles and petrified forests. In Mammoth Country, mineral-laden hot springs sculpt spectacular tiers of cascading stone terraces. In Lake Country, one of the largest alpine lakes in the world creates its own dramatic weather patterns.

Besides astonishing wildlife, pristine vistas, and geologic wonders, Yellowstone abounds with colorful history and has six National Historic Landmarks, including Old Faithful Inn and three architecturally significant museums designed by Herbert Maier. During the past twenty years, over fifty million people have visited this protected parkland that spreads across three states. No doubt they returned home feeling invigorated by the exuberance of nature and carrying with them unforgettable experiences.

WHITE BEAN PURÉE, BAKED SHIITAKE MUSHROOMS, AND ROASTED RED PEPPERS

White bean purée, spread on crostini or warm pita bread wedges and topped with baked shiitakes or roasted peppers, makes a sumptuous appetizer.

WHITE BEAN PURÉE

1 roasted garlic bulb (see Basics)

One 15-ounce can small white beans, drained and rinsed

1 tablespoon fresh lemon juice

$1/2$ teaspoon minced fresh rosemary

1 teaspoon salt

Freshly cracked pepper to taste

$1/3$ cup olive oil

BAKED SHIITAKE MUSHROOMS

8 ounces shiitake mushrooms, stemmed and thinly sliced

$1/2$ cup olive oil

1 tablespoon *each* minced fresh rosemary and thyme

1 teaspoon *each* salt and cracked pepper

ROASTED RED PEPPERS

2 red bell peppers, roasted, seeded, and finely diced (see Basics)

2 tablespoons extra-virgin olive oil

Crostini (see Basics), or warmed pita breads sliced into wedges, for serving

To make the white bean purée: In a food processor, combine the roasted garlic, white beans, lemon juice, rosemary, salt, pepper, and olive oil. Purée until smooth. Transfer to a serving bowl or ramekin.

To make the baked mushrooms: Preheat the oven to 400°F. In a medium bowl, toss the mushrooms with the olive oil, rosemary, thyme, salt, and pepper until thoroughly coated. Spread the mushrooms on a baking sheet and bake in the preheated oven for 20 to 25 minutes, or until crisp and fragrant. Transfer to a serving bowl or ramekin.

In a serving bowl, toss the peppers and olive oil together. *Makes 4 servings*

Climb the mountains and get their good tidings.

Nature's peace will flow into you as sunshine flows into trees.

The winds will blow their own freshness into you and

the storms their energy, while cares will drop off like autumn leaves.

—John Muir

DUCK BREAST ROULADE WITH COGNAC SAUCE, POLENTA, AND HARICOTS VERTS

Complementary flavors and textures are well balanced in this outstanding dish.

Polenta (recipe follows)

DUCK BREAST ROULADE

4 boneless duck breast halves with
skin, trimmed of excess fat
Salt and freshly cracked pepper to
taste
6 tablespoons finely chopped pistachios
or almonds
2 tablespoons ground dried porcini or
morel mushrooms

COGNAC SAUCE

Pan drippings, above
1 shallot, minced
1 garlic clove, minced

1 bay leaf
1 teaspoon brine-packed green peppercorns, rinsed
1 teaspoon minced fresh thyme
2 cups dry red wine
2 cups chicken stock (see Basics) or
canned low-salt chicken broth
2 tablespoons Cognac or brandy
2 tablespoons unsalted butter
Salt and freshly ground pepper to taste

HARICOTS VERTS

1 pound haricots verts or baby green
beans, trimmed
2 tablespoons unsalted butter at room
temperature
Salt and freshly cracked pepper to taste

To make the roulade: Slice each duck breast horizontally, until almost completely cut through but leaving the 2 halves still connected. Open each breast up and place between sheets of plastic wrap. Use a meat pounder to lightly pound until 1/4 inch thick. (If possible, have your butcher do this for you.)

Place the breasts, skin side down, on a work surface and sprinkle with salt and pepper. Place a heaping tablespoon of the nuts along one long side. Roll the meat up, like a jelly roll, into a roulade and secure with a few toothpicks. Coat the roulade all over with the ground mushrooms.

In a large ovenproof frying pan over low heat, cook the duck breasts, skin side down, for 8 minutes, or until crisp and golden brown. Pour off the fat, turn

(continued)

the breasts over, and continue cooking for 5 minutes for medium rare. Transfer to a cutting board, skin side up, and loosely cover with aluminum foil.

🍃 To make the Cognac sauce: Place the pan used to cook the duck breasts over medium heat and sauté the shallot for 2 minutes, or until golden. Add the garlic and sauté for 2 minutes. Add the bay leaf, peppercorns, thyme, and red wine. Increase heat to high and cook for about 10 minutes, or until reduced and syrupy. Add the chicken stock or broth and Cognac or brandy and cook until reduced by half, about 7 minutes. Remove from heat and strain the sauce through a fine-mesh sieve. Whisk in the butter and season with salt and pepper.

🍃 To make the haricots verts: In a large pot of salted boiling water, cook the haricots verts or green beans for 3 to 5 minutes, or until crisp-tender. Drain, transfer to a bowl, and toss with the butter, salt, and pepper.

🍃 Spoon a mound of polenta in the center of each of 4 warmed plates and arrange the haricots verts or green beans alongside. Thinly slice the duck roulade. Spoon the Cognac sauce below the polenta and fan out the duck slices over the sauce. Spoon a little sauce over the duck and serve immediately. *Makes 4 servings*

POLENTA

1 tablespoon olive oil
2 garlic cloves, minced
4 cups water
2 teaspoons salt
1¹/₄ cups polenta
1 teaspoon dried sage

²/₃ cup heavy cream or half-and-half
¹/₂ cup grated Parmesan cheese
2 tablespoons unsalted butter at
    room temperature
Salt and freshly cracked pepper to
    taste

🍃 In a small frying pan over medium heat, heat the olive oil and sauté the garlic for 2 minutes, or until fragrant. Set aside. In a large saucepan, bring the water to a boil. Add the salt. Gradually add the polenta, stirring constantly with a wooden spoon. Reduce heat to low and stir constantly for 10 minutes. Add the garlic, sage, and cream or half-and-half to the polenta and stir 10 minutes longer. Stir in the Parmesan cheese, butter, salt, and pepper. Cover and set aside. Just before serving, reheat over low heat, adding more water if the polenta is too thick. *Makes 4 servings*

ALBERT BIERSTADT *Upper Falls of the Yellowstone* 1872 The Lyle and Aileen Woodcock Museum

FRENCH CRUMB CAKE
WITH HUCKLEBERRY SAUCE

Serve this moist streusel-topped cake with huckleberry or blueberry sauce and vanilla ice cream. The huckleberry or blueberry sauce also makes a great topping for vanilla ice cream.

STREUSEL TOPPING

1/2 cup sugar

1 cup all-purpose flour

1 teaspoon ground cinnamon

1/2 cup (1 stick) cold unsalted butter, cut into small pieces

CAKE

1 cup (2 sticks) unsalted butter at room temperature

1 1/3 cups sugar

3/4 teaspoon salt

3 eggs

2 3/4 cups all-purpose flour

1 1/4 teaspoons baking powder

1 cup milk

1 teaspoon vanilla extract

Huckleberry Sauce (recipe follows)

Vanilla ice cream for serving

To make the streusel topping: In a medium bowl, combine the sugar, flour, and cinnamon. Add the butter and use your fingers to rub it into the mixture until it resembles coarse crumbs. Set aside.

To make the cake: Preheat the oven to 375°F. Butter and flour a 9-inch square cake pan.

In a large bowl, beat the butter, sugar, and salt together until pale and fluffy. Add the eggs and beat until pale, about 3 minutes.

In a small bowl, combine the flour and baking powder. Stir the flour mixture into the butter mixture until just incorporated. Stir in the milk and vanilla to make a smooth batter; do not overmix.

Pour the cake batter into the prepared pan. Smooth the top and sprinkle evenly with the streusel topping. Bake in the preheated oven for 40 minutes, or until a skewer inserted in the center comes out clean. Remove and let cool on a wire rack.

To serve, slice the cake into 3-inch squares, spoon over the huckleberry sauce, and top with a scoop of vanilla ice cream. *Makes one 9-inch square cake*

THOMAS MORAN *Tower Falls and Sulphur Mountain, Yellowstone* c. 1875

HUCKLEBERRY SAUCE

Fresh, bright-tasting huckleberries are found in summer produce markets in areas where they grow wild. Similar to blueberries, huckleberries are smaller and have more-noticeable seeds. Blueberries may be substituted.

2 cups fresh or frozen huckleberries or
   blueberries
$3/4$ cup sugar

1 cup water
$1/2$ cup port

In a medium saucepan, combine all the ingredients. Bring to a boil over high heat. Reduce heat to medium and simmer for 15 minutes, or until syrupy; use the back of a wooden spoon to break up the berries. Remove from heat and let cool. The sauce will thicken as it cools. If using huckleberries, strain the sauce through a fine-mesh sieve before serving. *Makes about 3 cups*

LAKE YELLOWSTONE HOTEL

JENNY LAKE LODGE
GRAND TETON NATIONAL PARK

A historic log lodge and five cabins still remain as part of beloved Jenny Lake Lodge, which originally opened in the 1920s as a dude ranch built by bachelor cowboy Tony Grace. His Danny Ranch sat on land at the base of the Tetons and was as close as private property could be to beautiful Jenny Lake. Today, guests return year after year to enjoy luxury, rusticity, and peacefulness at this Mobil Four-Star and AAA four-diamond property.

In 1872, Congress sent the Hayden survey party to the Grand Teton region. Members of the expedition included photographer William Henry Jackson and esteemed painter Thomas Moran. Photographs and paintings by these two men inspired Americans and Europeans to visit the Tetons, and Congress was so impressed with Hayden's report that the forest surrounding Jenny Lake was included in the Teton Forest Reserve.

During the years before World War I, most settlers in the Teton region were cattle ranchers, but following the war some locals opened dude ranches. At Tony Grace's Danny Ranch, paying guests enjoyed big-game hunting, fishing, pack trips, and ranch parties. Jenny Lake became a famous fishing spot for cutthroat trout, and in 1921 an amazing thirty-five-pound trout was taken from the lake. Tony Grace sold his ranch in 1930 to the Snake River Land Company, which was owned by John D. Rockefeller, Jr. In 1937, park officials approved the use of Danny Ranch as a guest facility in the Grand Teton National Forest, and the ranch was renovated and renamed Jenny Lake Ranch.

Today, Jenny Lake Lodge is a rustically elegant resort with an inviting main lodge and thirty-seven Old West–style cabins set in a pine forest. Connected by winding pathways, the cozy cabins are plush with down comforters and handmade quilts, and each has a front porch with relaxing rocking chairs. Prominent Jenny Lake Lodge guests have included Princess Grace of Monaco and President Carter, who rode horses here with his family when they visited the valley in the 1970s.

MENU

Roasted Asparagus with Truffle-Mustard Potato Salad

Seared Scallops with Bacon-Roasted Fingerlings and Rosemary Oil

Apricot Bavarian Creams with Strawberry-Champagne Soup

Nightly rates at Jenny Lake Lodge include breakfast, a five-course dinner, horseback riding, and bicycling. There are three lakes within easy walking distance and miles of scenic hiking trails. Guests can enjoy float trips down the Snake River and golf at nearby Jackson Hole Golf & Tennis Club, ranked the best course in Wyoming. Local guides take anglers fishing on Jackson Lake and fly fishing on the area's many streams and rivers.

Jenny Lake's main lodge is a cozy spot for reading and playing games and is the setting for occasional chamber music concerts. The walls are hung with paintings by outstanding Jackson Hole artists, which continues the tradition of displaying local art that was established by John D. Rockefeller, Jr.

In Jenny Lake's award-winning dining room, visitors enjoy seasonal five-course dinners. Chef Wes Hamilton's exciting menus are reason enough to plan a stay at the lodge, and the restaurant's wine list has won the *Wine Spectator*'s Award of Excellence. After dinner, diners can relax in the front room, where the moose head above the fireplace, shot by the wife of the first governor of Wyoming, presides regally over all. Jenny Lake Lodge is immensely popular from the day it opens in early June until the season's end in early October. Chef Wes Hamilton created the following recipes and presented them to Menus and Music.

JENNY LAKE LODGE

ROASTED ASPARAGUS WITH TRUFFLE-MUSTARD POTATO SALAD

Crisp, bright green asparagus with a mustardy potato salad makes a delicious first course for a spring dinner. Roasting is a great way to capture the best asparagus flavor and texture.

2 bunches asparagus, trimmed
  (2 to 2$1/2$ pounds total)
2 tablespoons extra-virgin olive oil
Salt and freshly ground pepper to taste

TRUFFLE-MUSTARD POTATO SALAD
8 to 10 fingerling or small Yukon Gold
  potatoes, scrubbed and diced

3 tablespoons rice wine vinegar
1 teaspoon Dijon mustard
1 tablespoon sugar
$1/2$ tablespoon white truffle oil
1 garlic clove, minced
1 shallot, minced
$1/2$ cup extra-virgin olive oil
Salt and freshly ground pepper to taste

Preheat the oven to 450°F. In a large bowl, toss the asparagus with the olive oil, salt, and pepper. Spread the asparagus on a baking sheet lined with aluminum foil and bake for 7 minutes, or until crisp-tender.

To make the salad: In a medium saucepan, boil the potatoes in lightly salted water for 10 minutes, or until tender when pieced with a knife; drain and let cool. Cut the potatoes into bite-sized pieces.

In a medium bowl, whisk together the vinegar, mustard, sugar, truffle oil, garlic, shallot, olive oil, salt, and pepper.

In a medium bowl, combine the potatoes and $1/3$ cup of the mustard vinaigrette; reserve the remaining vinaigrette for another salad. Arrange 4 or 5 asparagus spears and a scoop of potato salad on each of 4 plates. *Makes 4 servings*

SEARED SCALLOPS WITH BACON-ROASTED FINGERLINGS AND ROSEMARY OIL

Rosemary-and-thyme-infused potatoes are smashed with tasty bits of chopped bacon to make a flavorful bed for seared scallops.

BACON-ROASTED FINGERLINGS

4 bacon slices

2 cups kosher salt

1 pound fingerling potatoes or small
Yukon Gold potatoes, scrubbed

1 sprig *each* fresh rosemary and fresh
thyme

1/4 cup heavy cream or half-and-half,
plus more as needed

2 tablespoons unsalted butter

Salt and freshly ground pepper to taste

ROSEMARY OIL

Leaves from 1 sprig fresh rosemary

1/4 cup chopped fresh spinach

1/2 cup extra-virgin olive oil

1/2 teaspoon salt

12 sea scallops

Salt and freshly ground pepper to taste

2 tablespoons olive oil

To make the potatoes: Preheat the oven to 350°F. In a medium frying pan over low heat, fry the bacon until almost crisp; transfer to paper towels to drain. Make a layer of the salt in a medium casserole. Arrange the potatoes in a single layer on top of the salt. Cover with the rosemary, thyme, and bacon slices. Cover the casserole and bake in the preheated oven for 1 hour. Remove the bacon and chop. Transfer the potatoes to a medium bowl. Add the bacon, the 1/4 cup cream or half-and-half, and the butter and smash with a large fork or a potato masher. Season with salt and pepper, adding more cream if necessary. Set aside and cover to keep warm.

To make the rosemary oil: In a blender, combine all the ingredients and purée until smooth.

Pat the scallops dry with paper towels. Sprinkle the scallops with salt and pepper. In a large frying pan over medium-high heat, heat the olive oil and sauté the scallops until golden brown, about 2 minutes on each side.

Spoon a mound of potatoes in the center of each of 4 warmed plates. Top the potatoes with 3 scallops and decorate the plate with dots of rosemary oil; serve immediately. *Makes 4 servings*

APRICOT BAVARIAN CREAMS
WITH STRAWBERRY-CHAMPAGNE SOUP

A bright-tasting fruit soup is the perfect foil for the molded cream that is the centerpiece of this elegant dessert. Serve with Champagne.

APRICOT BAVARIAN CREAMS

1 teaspoon unflavored gelatin
$1/2$ cup cold water
2 egg yolks
$1/4$ cup sugar
1 cup milk
$1/4$ cup apricot jam
1 cup heavy cream

STRAWBERRY-CHAMPAGNE SOUP

1 pint fresh strawberries, hulled
$1/2$ cup corn syrup
Seeds scraped from $1/2$ split vanilla
     bean, or 1 teaspoon vanilla extract
2 cups chilled Champagne

4 orange zest strips and fresh mint
     sprigs for garnish

To make the apricot Bavarian creams: In a small bowl, sprinkle the gelatin over the water; set aside and let soak.

In a double boiler, combine the egg yolks and sugar. Using an electric mixer, beat until the mixture is pale and doubled in volume.

In a small saucepan, heat the milk over low heat until bubbles form around the edges of the pan. Gradually beat the hot milk into the egg mixture. Pour the custard into a double boiler and cook over barely simmering water, stirring constantly, until slightly thickened. Remove from heat and whisk in the apricot jam and gelatin mixture. Let cool, then refrigerate the custard until thickened, at least 2 hours, stirring occasionally.

In a deep bowl, beat the cream until soft peaks form. Fold the whipped cream into the chilled custard. Pour the mixture into six $1/2$-cup molds and refrigerate until completely chilled and set, at least 2 hours.

To make the soup: In a food processor, combine the strawberries, corn syrup, and vanilla bean seeds or vanilla extract and purée. Transfer the strawberry mixture to a bowl, stir in the Champagne, and refrigerate until chilled, at least 2 hours.

Just before serving, unmold a Bavarian cream into the center of each of 4 bowls. Pour the chilled soup around the cream. Garnish the Bavarian cream with orange zest and a mint sprig and serve at once. *Makes 6 servings*

GRAND TETON NATIONAL PARK

MOOSE, WYOMING

Holding some of America's most mystically beautiful mountains and lakes, protecting an amazing range of animal and plant species, and offering a myriad of recreational opportunities, Grand Teton National Park encompasses nearly 310,000 acres. Although this park emerged from a complicated and controversial series of events, it now includes the Teton Range, Jackson Hole, a fifty-mile stretch of the Snake River, a dozen mountain glaciers, and many alpine lakes. Each year, the park attracts almost 4 million visitors who come to enjoy its abundant treasures.

Originally, Shoshone, Crow, Blackfeet, and other Native Americans camped in the valley at the base of the mountains during the summer, but none of these tribes made it their permanent home year-round. In the early 1800s, French Canadian trappers discovered the region, and since the mountains reminded them of the female anatomy, they called the three largest peaks they saw *les trois tétons*, "the three breasts."

In 1872, Congress financed the Hayden expedition to explore the Teton region. William Henry Jackson was a member of the Hayden party and took the first photographs of the Tetons. After 1900, the area gained a reputation as big-game country and tourism became a thriving business in the valley. Today remnants of abandoned dude ranches can still be seen in the park. By the 1920s, unsightly commercialization threatened the beautiful region. In 1929, President Calvin Coolidge signed a bill that created Grand Teton National Park, but only the Teton Range and six glacial lakes at the base of the peaks were protected.

From this point on, the philanthropic dedication of John D. Rockefeller, Jr., had a major role in creating the expansive park we enjoy today. Rockefeller traveled to Jackson Hole in 1924 and 1926 and was persuaded by arguments made by Yellowstone Park superintendent Horace Albright that something must be done to protect the valley. Rockefeller decided to purchase valley properties with the intention of donating the lands for National Park designation. Between 1928 and 1943, Rockefeller's Snake River Land Company bought more than 35,000 acres. Intense local hostility

surrounded these land acquisitions, and attempts by Rockefeller to give the properties to the National Park Service met resistance. After holding the land for fifteen years, Rockefeller became impatient with the stalemate surrounding the acceptance of his gift. In 1943, President Franklin Roosevelt used his power to proclaim Rockefeller's land on the valley floor as Jackson Hole National Monument. After World War II, local citizens began to realize that tourism offered an economic future for Jackson Hole. In 1950, President Harry Truman signed a bill that finally merged the 1929 National Park with the 1943 National Monument. This moment marked a notable conservation victory.

The dazzling Teton Range dominates the park landscape, with twelve Teton peaks reaching above 12,000 feet. Although this is the youngest range in the Rockies, the mountains display some of North America's oldest rocks. Here, two rectangular blocks of the earth's crust moved in different directions, one swinging upwards to form the mountains and the other hinging downwards to form the valley. This movement accounts for the region's abruptly dramatic juxtaposition of mountains and valley. The scenic Snake River threads the valley floor, flowing through Jackson Lake and eventually into the Columbia River. Although the Snake isn't a challenging whitewater ride, meandering float trips offer sightings of some of the area's exciting wildlife, including elk, moose, pronghorn, and bald eagles. Visitors can join a National Park Service ranger for visitor-center talks, hikes, and evening programs. There are over 200 miles of trails, and the Tetons offer many opportunities for climbers and mountaineers. Jackson Lake spans about sixteen miles and provides fishing, sailboating, and windsurfing. There are guided horseback rides through the park, and of course the startling beauty of the area makes it a photographer's paradise.

Hopefully, visitors to Grand Teton National Park will set aside time to take a long look at the glorious mountains, to gaze at the astonishing night sky in this region with little ambient light, and to enjoy the rare natural silence in a park that is blessedly one of the quietest places in the continental United States.

JACKSON LAKE LODGE
GRAND TETON NATIONAL PARK

During the early 1800s, explorers and fur trappers followed rivers west into uncharted wilderness and discovered the stunning beauty of the Grand Teton region. When big-game hunters from the East Coast and Europe visited the area during the early 1900s, they roughed it in tents or simple log cabins. By the 1920s, dude ranches were popular, and folks from the city paid for the privilege of living primitively and working beside the region's real cowboys. Other city dwellers came just to see the wondrous Tetons, and many of them were appalled by the lack of comfortable accommodations.

MENU

*Duck Prosciutto with
Caramelized Pears and
Balsamic Glaze*

*Pork Chops and Sausage
with Red Cabbage and Apples*

*Mocha Flans with Caramel Sauce
and English Toffee*

In 1922, the Amoretti family built an inn with modern conveniences for affluent tourists near the site of today's Jackson Lake Lodge. In 1926, John D. Rockefeller, Jr. and his family spent several nights at the Amoretti Inn. Rockefeller had fallen in love with the beauty of the area and was persuaded by Yellowstone superintendent Horace Albright to help preserve and protect the valley. He decided to purchase private properties with the intention of donating the land for National Park designation. Amoretti changed the name of his inn to Jackson Lake Lodge in the late 1920s, and Rockefeller's Snake River Land Company purchased the lodge in 1930. Rockefeller's company managed and operated the lodge until the mid-1950s, when it was apparent that visitor facilities in Grand Teton National Park were inadequate to meet booming demand. In 1953, based on financing assured by the Rockefellers, a lease agreement was reached between Rockefeller's management company and the National Park Service for land on which a new Jackson Lake Lodge would be built.

The building of the new Jackson Lake Lodge was an enormous undertaking. Situated on a bluff overlooking Jackson Lake that was selected by Rockefeller, the lodge was designed by Gilbert Stanley Underwood. Underwood had previously designed Bryce Canyon Lodge, Grand Canyon Lodge, and the Ahwahnee Hotel, but his bold design at Jackson

Lake was quite different from these rustic log-and-stone structures. Influenced by architectural style of the 1950s, his massive main lodge is 630 feet long, and its striking contemporary design features the use of reinforced concrete and a bank of enormous picture windows. These sixty-foot-tall glass panes in the lobby and the dining room frame spectacular views of the Tetons. When the lodge formally opened in 1955, it was filled with Western art that had been collected and commissioned by the Rockefellers. Today, the lodge has an eclectic collection of original Indian and trapper artifacts, photographs of early Jackson Hole residents, and contemporary artwork by outstanding local Jackson Hole artists. In 1989, Jackson Lake Lodge was the chosen setting for the signing of an agreement to end the Cold War between the Soviet Union and the United States. Since its opening, Jackson Lake Lodge has accommodated millions of visitors, and prominent past guests include President Kennedy, Lady Bird Johnson, President Nixon, President Reagan, and President Clinton.

Jackson Lake Lodge has 385 comfortable guest rooms in the main lodge and adjacent buildings. Lodge guests can enjoy walks and hikes, and the likelihood of seeing some of the park's exciting and abundant wildlife, especially at dawn and dusk. There are guided float trips on the scenic Snake River and golf at nearby Jackson Hole Golf & Tennis Club, ranked the best course in Wyoming. Local guides take anglers fishing on Jackson Lake and fly-fishing on the area's many streams and rivers. Many enjoy guided horseback excursions through the park, and there are informative programs by rangers, as well as narrated bus tours that introduce the area's geology and history. At nearby Colter Bay Village, the National Park Service operates the Visitor Center as wells as the Indian Arts Museum and Amphitheater. Nearby is the National Museum of Wildlife Art, a fine arts museum with a collection of wildlife art that is unsurpassed in the United States.

Even by national park standards, the views from the lodge dining room are breathtaking, and the restaurant is a splendid place to enjoy fine dining. The spacious Mural Room is named after the murals by Carl Roters that line the room. In 1957, by John D. Rockefeller, Jr. commissioned Roters to create large panels for the dining room, and the artist based his work on Alfred Jacob Miller's 1837 watercolor sketches of a fur trappers' "rendezvous." Executive chef Joseph A. Santangini's generous seasonal menus feature classic and Rocky Mountain cuisine. Chef Santangini created the following recipes and presented them to Menus and Music.

Open from mid-May to early October, Jackson Lake Lodge offers a spacious, informal place to relax in the heart of Grand Teton National Park.

CARL RUNGIUS *Wind River Bugler* 1923 National Museum of Wildlife Art

Our environment is part of us. How we care for our environment and live

with it, utilize and enjoy it, determines the kind of people we will be.

—Laurance S. Rockefeller

DUCK PROSCIUTTO
WITH CARAMELIZED PEARS
AND BALSAMIC GLAZE

This fabulous appetizer combines salty, sweet, smoky, and piquant flavors. Boneless, skinless chicken breasts are a good substitute for the duck breasts.

BRINE

4 cups water

$1/2$ cup packed brown sugar

$1/2$ cup salt

2 tablespoons whole allspice berries

1 tablespoon dill seed

2 tablespoons peppercorns

1 cinnamon stick

BALSAMIC GLAZE

1 cup balsamic vinegar

3 tablespoons unsalted butter

2 pears, peeled, cored, and each cut
  into 4 wedges

2 tablespoons sugar

Freshly ground pepper to taste

4 boneless, skinless duck breast halves

$1/2$ cup cedar-wood chips or mesquite
  smoking chips

🦆 In a stockpot, combine all the brine ingredients and bring to a boil. Add the duck breasts. Remove from heat and let cool. Refrigerate for 6 hours.

🦆 Prepare a fire in a charcoal grill. Soak the wood chips in water to cover for 30 minutes. Drain the wood chips and sprinkle over the coals. Place the duck on the grill, cover, and smoke the duck for 30 minutes.

🦆 Alternatively, line a wok or large cast-iron frying pan with heavy-duty aluminum foil, allowing the excess foil to hang over the sides. Place the duck breasts in a wire steamer basket that fits inside the wok or frying pan. Cover the wok or frying pan with a lid and place over high heat until smoke seeps out. Working quickly, uncover the wok or frying pan and place the rack with the duck inside. Cover and seal with the overhanging foil. Remove from heat and set aside; do not disturb for 30 minutes.

🍂 Remove the duck breasts and thinly slice on the diagonal.

🍂 To make the balsamic glaze: In a small saucepan over high heat, boil the balsamic vinegar until it becomes syrupy; set aside.

🍂 In a large frying pan, melt the butter over medium-high heat and add the pears. Sprinkle the pears with the sugar and cook for 2 minutes on each side, or until golden brown. Place 2 pear wedges on each of 4 plates. Thinly slice the pear wedges and fan out the slices. Sprinkle the pears with pepper and arrange 2 or 3 slices of smoked duck alongside. Garnish each plate with dots or drizzles of balsamic glaze and serve at once. *Makes 4 servings*

PORK CHOPS AND SAUSAGE
WITH RED CABBAGE AND APPLES

Piquant red cabbage and apples complement the rich flavor of pork.

4 thick pork loin chops

1/4 cup extra-virgin olive oil

2 garlic cloves, minced

1 teaspoon minced fresh rosemary

2 tablespoons dried green peppercorns, crushed

RED CABBAGE AND APPLES

1 1/2 tablespoons olive oil

1 onion, diced

6 cups thinly sliced red cabbage (about 1 small cabbage)

2 apples, peeled, cored, and cut into bite-sized pieces

1/2 cup water

2 tablespoons balsamic vinegar

2 tablespoons red wine vinegar

1 teaspoon salt

4 fresh pork sausages

Put the pork chops in a shallow roasting pan just large enough to hold them. Combine the olive oil, garlic, and rosemary in a small bowl and pour the marinade over the chops. Let stand at room temperature for 30 minutes.

Spread the crushed peppercorns on a plate or a sheet of waxed paper. Remove the pork from the marinade and coat the meat with the peppercorns.

Prepare a fire in a charcoal grill. While the coals are heating, make the red cabbage: In a large frying pan over medium heat, heat the olive oil and sauté the onion and cabbage for 5 minutes. Add the apples, water, balsamic vinegar, red wine vinegar, and salt. Cook, stirring occasionally, for 20 minutes, or until the cabbage is tender. Set aside and keep warm.

Grill the pork chops for about 7 minutes on each side, or until an instant-read thermometer registers 160°F. Using a fork, prick the sausage in several places. Grill the sausages, turning several times, until well browned and firm, about 10 minutes. Transfer to a cutting board, let cool, and slice on the diagonal.

TUCKER SMITH *Wyoming Range, Antelope* 1995 National Museum of Wildlife Art

🌿 Alternatively, heat a large, heavy frying pan, preferably cast iron, over high heat for 60 seconds. Remove the chops from the marinade and cook them for about 7 minutes on each side, or until cooked through but not dry. Brown the sausages on all sides until nicely browned and cooked through, about 10 minutes. Transfer to a cutting board, let cool, and slice on the diagonal.

🌿 Place a mound of red cabbage in the center of each of 4 warmed plates. Arrange a pork chop over the cabbage with sausage slices alongside; serve immediately. *Makes 4 servings*

MOCHA FLANS WITH
CARAMEL SAUCE AND ENGLISH TOFFEE

As dramatic as it is delicious, this dessert is good for a dinner party because it can be prepared almost entirely ahead. Crush some of the English toffee garnish and break the rest into jagged pieces that resemble the peaks of the Grand Tetons.

ENGLISH TOFFEE

1 cup sugar

$^1/_2$ cup (1 stick) unsalted butter

2 tablespoons water

1 teaspoon vanilla extract

CARAMEL SAUCE

$^3/_4$ cup sugar

$^1/_4$ cup water

$^1/_2$ cup heavy cream

FLAN

1$^3/_4$ cups heavy cream

6 tablespoons sugar

2 egg yolks

2 eggs

1 teaspoon Nutella (chocolate-hazelnut paste)

2 tablespoons cold brewed espresso or strong black coffee

To make the toffee: Place a baking sheet on a counter. In a small, heavy saucepan combine all the ingredients. Bring to a boil over medium-high heat and cook until golden brown, or until a candy thermometer inserted into the mixture registers 300°F. Immediately pour onto the pan. Let cool completely. Crush some of the toffee and break the rest into pieces.

To make the caramel sauce: In a small, heavy saucepan, combine the sugar and water. Bring to a boil over high heat and cook until golden brown. Immediately remove from heat and gradually whisk in the cream; take care, as it will spatter. Set aside.

To make the flan: Preheat the oven to 350°F. Butter four $^1/_2$-cup ramekins. In a medium, heavy saucepan, combine the cream and sugar. Bring to a boil over medium-high heat; remove from heat.

🍂 In a medium bowl, whisk the egg yolks and eggs until pale. Gradually whisk in the hot cream mixture. Return to the pan and stir in the Nutella and espresso or coffee. Cook over medium-low heat, stirring constantly, until thick enough to coat the back of a spoon. Pour the custard into the prepared ramekins and place in a large baking dish. Add hot water to come halfway up the sides of the ramekins. Bake in the preheated oven for 20 to 25 minutes, or until the custard is just set; the centers will jiggle slightly. Let cool. Refrigerate the flans until chilled, at least 2 hours or up to 24 hours.

🍂 Just before serving, run a knife around the outside of each custard. Gently unmold a flan onto each of 4 plates. Spoon over a little warm caramel sauce and garnish with toffee pieces and crushed toffee. *Makes 4 servings*

SUNDANCE

SUNDANCE, UTAH

Created as a community for artistic growth, recreation, and cherishing the wilderness, Sundance is a place for guests to enjoy year-round outdoor activities, rustically luxurious accommodation, and fine dining. Set on 6,000 acres of protected land, this gorgeous sanctuary is a dream that Robert Redford has carefully nurtured for more than three decades.

Sundance nestles in a canyon on the slopes of 12,000 foot Mount Timpanogos, the highest point in the Wasatch Range. Centuries ago, the Ute Indians retreated to the canyon to escape the summer heat and hunt game. By the beginning of the twentieth century, the Stewarts, a family of Scottish immigrants, settled in the canyon and used some of the land as sheep pasture. The second generation of Stewarts operated a small ski resort and a burger joint until 1969, when Robert Redford purchased the resort and much of the surrounding land. He hoped to preserve the natural beauty of the area and to develop a small, sustainable community for lovers of nature and the arts. In the beginning, it was nearly impossible to get people to invest in this dream, but today Sundance is not only a successful resort, it is also an arts institute, a catalog, and a film festival.

In 1981, Sundance Canyon became the birthplace of the Sundance Institute. Founded to support artistic vitality and diversity in American filmmaking, the Institute's film festival is held in nearby Park City and has grown to become the nation's premier showcase for independent filmmakers. At the Sundance Institute, playwrights, moviemakers, writers, composers, actors, and musicians work in an inspiring setting surrounded by nature. Every summer, Sundance guests and community audiences enjoy professional theater under the stars, children's matinees, concerts, and other cultural events.

Overnight guest accommodations, carefully designed to blend with the landscape, were built beginning in 1988 and finally completed in 1996. Today, Sundance Village has

---

MENU

*Roasted Beets and
Three-Bean Salad with
Mustard Vinaigrette*

*Grilled Venison Rack
with Huckleberry Sauce,
Braised Chard, and
Butternut Squash Purée*

*Warm Chocolate Cakes with
Chocolate Ice Cream*

ninety-five guest cottages, privately owned mountain homes, shops, restaurants, a rehearsal/concert/performance hall, a screening room, an artisan center, and a conference facility tucked into the forest at the base of the ski mountain.

All the guest cottages have an atmosphere of rustic luxury, and their cozy interiors include rough-sawn beams, plush down comforters, Native American art, and stone fireplaces or woodstoves. Just steps away from Sundance Village, they have easy access to the ski lifts, the old-fashioned Sundance General Store that is the inspiration for the Sundance catalog, and the Art Shack Studios. At this artisan center, professional artists and teachers offer classes in painting, pottery, photography, jewelry making, and drawing.

Outdoor recreation is enjoyed during every season at Sundance. In winter, it is one of the most beautiful settings in the Rockies and draws serious skiers who enjoy Utah's famous powder. The relatively uncrowded slopes are family friendly and suitable for skiers of all abilities. There are miles of groomed cross-country and snowshoe trails through the alpine meadows and aspen groves of Elk Meadows Preserve. In summer, guests enjoy hiking, horseback riding, mountain biking, and fly-fishing. In any season, guests can join yoga classes in the yoga yurt or relax as they receive natural therapies, massage, and herbal skin care treatments in the spa.

At the casual Foundry Grill, fresh, flavorful New West cuisine is served for breakfast, lunch, and dinner. The restaurant has a wood-burning grill, oven, and rotisserie, and features a selection of grilled meats. Next door, the Owl Bar has a restored 1890s rosewood bar that was moved from Thermopolis, Wyoming and once served Butch Cassidy's Hole-in-the-Wall Gang.

The award-winning Tree Room is an enchanting art-filled restaurant for fine dining. The wood-paneled room is decorated with Native American baskets, rugs, and ceramics and memorabilia from Robert Redford's personal collection. The room was built around a seventy-foot pine tree, and although the tree died two years after the restaurant opened in 1970, Redford kept it in place because it "symbolized the fights I waged to get the place built." Chef Jason Knibb bases his seasonal mountain cuisine on fresh organically grown produce and naturally raised meats and fowl. He uses produce from Sundance Farms and other local farmers as much as possible. On weekends after dinner, guests can watch films in the Screening Room that were created at the Sundance Institute or that came to prominence at the Sundance Film Festival. Chef Jason Knibb created the following recipes and presented them to Menus and Music.

Whether guests come to ski, hike, write, or simply to relax, they find an unspoiled sanctuary where their spirits can soar. Sundance is a place with heart and soul that is on a steady, naturally beautiful course of its own.

To us, Sundance is and always will be a dream.

What you see, smell, taste, and feel here is a dream being carefully nurtured.

—Robert Redford

ROASTED BEETS AND THREE-BEAN SALAD WITH MUSTARD VINAIGRETTE

Roasting beets concentrates and rounds out their delicious flavor. This salad balances the flavors of sweet beets, nutty green beans and arugula, and a mustardy vinaigrette.

6 baby Chiogga beets, greens trimmed to 1 inch
1 pound mixed haricots verts, yellow wax beans, and Romano beans, trimmed

MUSTARD VINAIGRETTE
$1/2$ cup Champagne or sherry vinegar
1 tablespoon Dijon mustard
$3/4$ cup extra-virgin olive oil
Salt and freshly ground pepper to taste

8 ounces baby arugula leaves
1 shallot, minced
$1/2$ cup pine nuts, toasted (see Basics)

🌱 Preheat the oven to 350°F. Put the beets in a baking dish with 1 cup water, cover the dish with aluminum foil, and bake in the preheated oven for 30 to 40 minutes, or until the beets are tender when pierced with a knife. Remove from the oven and let cool. Gently rub the beets with paper towels to remove the skins, or use a small sharp knife to slice off the skins.

🌱 While the beets are roasting, cook the beans in a large pot of salted boiling water for 4 minutes, or until crisp-tender (add the larger beans first). Drain into a colander and run the beans under cold water to stop the cooking process; set aside.

🌱 To make the vinaigrette: In a small bowl, whisk the vinegar and mustard together. Gradually whisk in the olive oil, salt, and pepper. Remove and reserve $1/4$ cup of the vinaigrette.

🌱 Using a sharp knife or mandoline, thinly slice the beets. Arrange the slices in a circle on each of 4 salad plates. Brush the beets with a little of the mustard vinaigrette. In 2 medium bowls, separately toss the arugula, shallot, and pine nuts, and the haricots, yellow wax beans, and Romano beans, with half the mustard vinaigrette. Arrange a mound of arugula salad in the center of each beet circle and pile the beans on top. Drizzle 1 tablespoon of the reserved vinaigrette around each plate and serve at once. *Makes 4 servings*

GRILLED VENISON RACK WITH HUCKLEBERRY SAUCE, BRAISED CHARD, AND BUTTERNUT SQUASH PURÉE

This flavorful dish can also be made with pork loin. The meat is best cooked to medium rare, since most game toughens if cooked above 135°F. Have your butcher "French" the rack by removing the meat and fat from the top inch or so of the rib bones.

1 rack of venison*, frenched and
  trimmed of fat (reserve trimmings)
$^1/_2$ carrot, peeled and diced
1 celery stalk, diced
1 small onion, chopped
4 garlic cloves, smashed
Leaves from 1 sprig *each* fresh thyme,
  sage, and parsley, chopped
$^1/_2$ cup dry red wine

$^1/_2$ cup port
1 tablespoon olive oil, plus oil for coating
6 cups chicken stock (see Basics) or
  canned low-salt chicken broth
$^1/_2$ cup fresh or frozen huckleberries or
  blueberries
Salt and freshly ground pepper to taste
Braised Swiss Chard (recipe follows)
Butternut Squash Purée (recipe follows)

🌿 Put the venison rack in a glass baking dish. Add the carrot, celery, onion, garlic, herbs, red wine, and port and let stand at from temperature for 2 hours, turning occasionally. Transfer the venison to a plate. Strain the vegetables; reserve the liquid and vegetables separately.

🌿 To make the huckleberry sauce: In a large saucepan over medium-high heat, heat the 1 tablespoon olive oil until almost smoking. Add the reserved trimmings and sauté until browned, about 5 minutes. Transfer the trimmings to a bowl and set aside. Add the reserved vegetables and sauté for 10 minutes, or until browned. Pour in the reserved wine and boil to reduce to $^1/_4$ cup; skim off any foam that rises to the surface. Add the stock or broth, reduce heat to medium-low, and simmer the sauce for 1 hour, or until reduced to about 4 cups. Strain through a fine-mesh sieve into a bowl; discard the solids. Return to the saucepan, add the huckleberries or blueberries, and cook over medium-high heat for 20 minutes, or until the liquid is reduced to about 1$^1/_2$ cups. Season with salt and pepper.

🌿 Prepare a fire in a charcoal grill. Clean the grill rack and brush it with oil. Coat the venison with olive oil and sprinkle with salt and pepper. Place the venison rack, loin side down, on the grill and cook for 4 to 6 minutes. Turn and grill on the second side for 4 to 6 minutes, or until an instant-read thermometer inserted into the thickest part of the meat registers 130°F for medium rare; the venison will toughen if cooked over 135°F. Transfer to a plate and cover loosely with aluminum foil.

To serve, ladle 1/4 cup of the butternut squash into the center of each of 4 warmed plates. Using the ladle, spread the purée out to create a 4-inch diameter pool, and place a mound of braised Swiss chard in the center of each pool. Carve the venison rack into 4 double-cut chops and place 1 chop over each mound of chard. Spoon the huckleberry sauce around the squash purée. *Makes 4 servings*

*Venison racks and loins can be ordered from specialty meat markets or by mail order.

BRAISED SWISS CHARD

2 bacon slices
4 shallots, diced

2 bunches red Swiss chard, stemmed and chopped
Salt and freshly ground pepper to taste

In a large frying pan over medium heat, fry the bacon until crisp; transfer to paper towels to drain. In the same pan, sauté the shallots for 3 minutes, or until golden brown. Stir in the Swiss chard and cook for 5 to 7 minutes, or until tender. Season with salt and pepper. Serve warm. *Makes 4 servings*

BUTTERNUT SQUASH PURÉE

1 butternut squash
1/4 cup olive oil

1 tablespoon salt
1/2 teaspoon ground pepper

Preheat the oven to 350°F. Cut the squash in half and remove the seeds. Peel and cut the squash into large dice. In a medium bowl, toss the butternut squash pieces with the olive oil, salt, and pepper until thoroughly coated.

Transfer the squash to a baking dish, cover with aluminum foil, and bake in the oven for 30 to 45 minutes, or until soft. Transfer the squash to a food processor and purée. Transfer the purée to a bowl and serve warm. *Makes 4 servings*

WARM CHOCOLATE CAKES
WITH CHOCOLATE ICE CREAM

Chocolate, chocolate, chocolate! Individual chocolate cakes served with creamy chocolate sauce and topped with smooth dark chocolate ice cream. Use the best-quality chocolate you can find.

CHOCOLATE CAKES

6 ounces bittersweet or semisweet
  chocolate, chopped
$3/4$ cup ($1^1/2$ sticks) unsalted butter
3 eggs
3 egg yolks
6 tablespoons all-purpose flour
6 tablespoons sugar

CHOCOLATE SAUCE

$2^1/4$ ounces bittersweet or semisweet
  chocolate, chopped
$1/2$ cup water
$1/4$ cup heavy cream
3 tablespoons sugar

Chocolate Ice Cream (recipe follows)

To make the chocolate cakes: Preheat the oven to 400°F. Butter six $1/2$-cup ramekins. In a medium saucepan, melt the chocolate and butter over very low heat; immediately remove from heat.

Using an electric mixer, beat the eggs and egg yolks together until pale and tripled in volume, about 7 minutes. In a small bowl, combine the flour and sugar. Stir to blend. Fold the flour mixture into the egg mixture. Fold in the warm chocolate mixture. Pour the batter into the prepared ramekins and bake in the preheated oven for 11 to 12 minutes, or until a skewer inserted in the center comes out almost clean.

To make the chocolate sauce: In a medium, heavy saucepan, combine all the ingredients and bring to a boil over medium heat, stirring constantly with a wooden spoon. Reduce heat to low and cook, stirring frequently, until the sauce thickens enough to coat the back of the spoon, about 10 minutes.

To serve: Spread about 2 tablespoons of the chocolate sauce into a pool in the center of each of 6 plates. Unmold the cakes and place one in the center of each pool of chocolate sauce. Place a scoop of the chocolate ice cream on top of each cake and serve. *Makes 6 servings*

CHOCOLATE ICE CREAM

3 tablespoons dry milk
1¹/₂ cups whole milk
3 tablespoons sugar

4 ounces bittersweet or semisweet
chocolate, chopped

Put the dry milk in a medium, heavy saucepan. Gradually whisk in the whole milk until dissolved. Whisk in the sugar. Bring the mixture to a boil over medium-high heat. Stir in the chocolate and bring to a boil again. Immediately remove from heat and let cool. Refrigerate until chilled, at least 2 hours. Freeze in an ice cream maker according to the manufacturer's instructions. Pack the ice cream into a freezer container and freeze for at least 2 hours. *Makes about 1 pint*

BRYCE CANYON LODGE

BRYCE CANYON NATIONAL PARK, UTAH

First-time guests at Bryce Canyon Lodge have no idea of the surprise that awaits them when they peer over the edge of the nearby canyon! Set just back from the rim of a dazzling natural amphitheater, the lodge has unsurpassed access to a fantastic throng of "hoodoos," pink-hued stone spires, fins, and pinnacles that resemble tall whimsical sculptures or a mad organist's pipe dream. The rustic lodge has been restored to its original 1920s look and is popular from the day it opens in April until the day it closes in October.

> ## MENU
>
> *Jalapeno-Hummus Dip*
>
> *Pan-Fried Red Trout Fillets*
>
> *Bryceberry Bread Pudding with Bourbon Sauce*

Bryce Canyon Lodge and its forty surrounding cabins were designed by architect Gilbert Stanley Underwood. The two-story lodge opened in 1924 and was built from locally harvested timber and quarried stone. Over the years, many changes were made to update the building and its original interior details were lost and so was its historic charm. Fortunately, during the late 1980s the lodge was extensively rehabilitated. Today, the lobby's wood paneling, stone fireplace, replicas of the original hickory furniture, and large log chandelier create a welcoming rustic-lodge atmosphere. On the second floor are the guest suites, while the first floor houses the dining room, a gift shop, a small post office, and an auditorium, in addition to the registration desk and lobby.

Just a short walk from the main lodge, are Western log cabins clustered in a Ponderosa pine forest near the rim. The cabins are prime examples of Underwood's rustic building style, and their steeply pitched roofs, log-framed private porches, and gas-log fireplaces create quiet, relaxing retreats.

From late spring through early fall, lodge guests enjoy walks and hikes, wrangler-guided horseback rides into the amphitheater, stargazing, and interpretive day and evening programs led by National Park Service rangers. Overlooks along the rim are especially scenic at sunrise and sunset, but the best way to see the hoodoos is by hiking the trails that descend into the amphitheater—just remember, the trails involve steep climbs out of the canyon! The popular Navajo Loop Trail winds through slot canyons, and the Queen's

Garden Trail passes exquisitely eroded rock formations, including one in the shape of Queen Victoria that is a favorite with English tourists. Each month during the full moon, there are moonlight hikes among the amazing hoodoos. Kids can join rangers for games and activities that teach them about Bryce Canyon and its ecology.

Bryce Canyon Lodge guests can enjoy breakfast, lunch, and dinner in a historic dining room. The white-pine-paneled room has exposed wood trusses, decorative forged-iron light fixtures, and a rough-stone fireplace that often has cozy fires. In the evening, the atmosphere and attire are casual, but tables are set with crisp white tablecloths. The dinner menu features Western and Southwestern dishes, and for dessert there is Bryceberry Bread Pudding (see page 142), a lodge specialty. Chef Les Garvin created the following recipes and presented them to Menus and Music.

An architecturally significant example of rustic park architecture, Bryce Canyon Lodge is set in a region of astonishing beauty and is one America's original national park lodges.

BRYCE CANYON NATIONAL PARK

UTAH

Bryce Canyon National Park is an extraordinary wonderland of stone. Each year, almost two million people visit the park to gaze at the colorful rock pinnacles and spires that stand like sentries against the blue Southwestern sky. Unlike nearby Grand Canyon and Zion National Parks, where deep canyons have been cut by rivers, Bryce Canyon is a series of natural amphitheaters created by ice, snow, and rain at the edge of southern Utah's Paunsaugunt Plateau. The beautiful rock figures for which Bryce is famous—called "hoodoos" by geologists—create a veritable forest of stone within the amphitheaters.

In the winter, melting snow seeps into cracks in the plateau's ancient layers of stone. About 200 times a year, in a process called "frost wedging," the melted snow freezes and expands, then thaws and contracts. These freeze/thaw cycles crack the stone apart until it separates into thin walls. The scant rainfall at Bryce slowly dissolves the layers of limestone, and the walls break apart into hoodoos. Mudstone and siltstone, more resistant to erosion, cause the strange, lumpy silhouettes that make the hoodoos so spectacular. The most durable rock formations are capped with a special kind of limestone called dolomite, which dissolves very slowly and protects the weaker stone below. Hoodoos have a limited lifespan, and Bryce's profile is constantly changing as old shapes crumble and new ones appear.

Scientists have discovered signs of human habitation near Bryce Canyon dating to almost 10,000 years ago. The Paiute people are among the region's more recent inhabitants, although they arrived hundreds of years before the first Europeans. According to a Paiute legend, Bryce's rock formations were created when Trickster Coyote became so angry at the Legend People, a pre-human race, that he turned them to stone. One translation of the Paiute name for Bryce Canyon is "Red Rocks Standing Like Men in a Bowl-Shaped Canyon."

Although European fur trappers and traders passed through southern Utah in the early 1800s, they left no records of having seen the area that is now Bryce Canyon National Park. In 1875, the Church of Latter Day Saints sent a carpenter named Ebenezer Bryce to the region, believing his skills would be useful in settling the area. The strange amphitheater near Ebenezer's home was called Bryce's Canyon by neighboring settlers. The "canyon" was first set aside as a national monument in 1923 and became a national park in 1924.

Bryce Canyon is home to a variety of wildlife, including mountain lions, mule deer, coyotes, and Utah prairie dogs, an endangered species. Bristlecone and pinyon pines are two notable trees that grow in the park. Bristlecones are known to live longer than almost any other tree in the world, and Bryce is home to one that is at least 1,600 years old. Pine nuts from pinyon trees were an important food source for the Paiute tribe and are still prized by modern-day cooks.

Park visitors can enjoy hikes along the amphitheater's rim while looking down at the strange world below. The breathtaking views are especially dramatic at sunrise and sunset, when golden light seems to set the rocks on fire. Many enjoy hikes within the amphitheater among the stone pinnacles, slot canyons, and arches. During popular full-moon night hikes, shadows bounce off the rocky shapes to create a beautiful, albeit spooky, atmosphere. There are shuttle bus tours to scenic viewpoints during the summer, and throughout the year, National Park Service rangers offer lectures and guided hikes. In winter, the snowcapped hoodoos are a magical sight, and free snowshoes can be borrowed at the visitor's center.

One meaning of the word *hoodoo*, "to cast a spell," is fitting, for visitors will never forget the enchanting world of stone at Bryce Canyon.

JALAPENO-HUMMUS DIP

Serve this spicy dip with tortilla chips, warm pita bread slices, or crudités such as baby carrots, radishes, broccoli and cauliflower florets, and cherry tomatoes.

2 tablespoons extra-virgin olive oil
1 tablespoon Asian (toasted) sesame oil
2 tablespoons fresh lemon juice
1 garlic clove, minced

One 15-ounce can garbanzo beans, drained and rinsed
1/2 small jalapeno chili, seeded and minced
Salt, freshly ground pepper, and Tabasco sauce to taste

🌿 In a blender or food processor, combine all the ingredients and purée. Transfer to a serving bowl. *Makes about 1 1/2 cups*

PAN-FRIED RED TROUT FILLETS

Delicious served with boiled new potatoes and a seasonal fresh vegetable.

1 teaspoon *each* ground cumin, chili powder, paprika, salt, pepper, and finely grated lemon zest (see Basics)
1/2 cup all-purpose flour

4 red trout fillets
2 tablespoons unsalted butter
4 sprigs fresh parsley and lemon wedges for garnish

🌿 In a small bowl, combine the spices, lemon zest, and flour. Spread the spice mixture on a large plate and lightly dredge each trout fillet on both sides in the mixture. Set aside.

🌿 In a large frying pan, melt the butter over medium-high heat and add the trout fillets just before the butter browns. Cook for 4 minutes on each side, or until golden brown. Transfer the fillets to each of 4 plates and garnish with parsley and lemon. Serve immediately. *Makes 4 servings*

BRYCEBERRY BREAD PUDDING
WITH BOURBON SAUCE

Moist bread pudding served with berry compote and a warm, creamy bourbon sauce.

BISCUITS

2 cups all-purpose flour

2 tablespoons sugar

3 teaspoons baking powder

1/2 teaspoon salt

1/2 cup (1 stick) cold unsalted butter,
cut into small pieces

1 egg

2/3 cup half-and-half

1/4 cup raisins

1/2 teaspoon ground cinnamon

1/4 teaspoon freshly grated nutmeg

2 tablespoons shredded coconut
(optional)

1 cup mixed fresh or frozen blueberries, raspberries, and blackberries

1 1/2 teaspoons vanilla extract

2 eggs, lightly beaten

1 1/2 cups heavy cream or half-and-half

BERRY COMPOTE

1 cup fresh or frozen blueberries

1 cup fresh or frozen raspberries

1 cup fresh or frozen blackberries

1/2 cup sugar

Bourbon Sauce (recipe follows)

To make the biscuits: Preheat the oven to 450°F. Butter a 9-inch square baking dish. In a large bowl, stir the flour, sugar, baking powder, and salt together. Add the butter and use a pastry cutter or 2 dinner knives to cut it in until the mixture resembles coarse crumbs. In a small bowl, whisk the egg and half-and-half together. Add the egg mixture to the flour mixture and stir with a fork until just combined; do not overmix the dough.

On a lightly floured work surface, knead the dough a few times, just until smooth. Pat or roll out the dough until 1/2 inch thick and cut into biscuits. Transfer for a baking sheet and bake in the preheated oven for 10 minutes, or until golden brown. Transfer to wire rack, let cool, and coarsely chop.

🍂 Preheat the oven to 350°F. In a large bowl, combine the chopped biscuits, raisins, cinnamon, nutmeg, and coconut, if using. In a medium bowl, combine the berries, vanilla, eggs, and cream or half-and-half. Pour the biscuit mixture into the berry mixture and stir just until blended. Pour the pudding into the prepared baking dish and bake for 45 minutes, or until golden brown.

🍂 To make the berry compote: In a medium saucepan, combine all the ingredients and cook over medium-high heat for 15 to 20 minutes, stirring frequently. Remove from heat and let cool to room temperature.

🍂 To serve, cut the pudding into squares. Top with berry compote, then spoon over some warm bourbon sauce. *Makes 6 to 8 servings*

BOURBON SAUCE

$^1/_2$ cup (1 stick) unsalted butter
$^1/_2$ cup packed brown sugar

1 cup heavy cream or half-and-half
2 tablespoons bourbon

🍂 In a small, heavy saucepan, melt the butter over medium heat. Add the sugar and cook until golden brown. Immediately remove from heat and stir in the cream; take care, as it will splatter. Let cool slightly. Stir in the bourbon and serve warm. *Makes about 2 cups*

When lighted by the morning sun the gorgeous chasm is an immense bowl of lace and filigree work in stone, colored with the white of frost and the pinks of glowing embers. To those who have not forgotten the story books of childhood it suggests a playground for fairies. In another aspect it seems a smoldering inferno where goblins and demons might dwell among flames and embers.

—The Union Pacific System

ZION LODGE

ZION NATIONAL PARK, UTAH

Guests on their way to Zion Lodge from the east entrance of the park follow a red asphalt road through an arid landscape with astounding rock formations, including immense and naturally sculpted Checkerboard Mesa. Continuing along the Zion–Mount Carmel Highway, and after emerging from a one-mile-long tunnel blasted through solid sandstone, they surely gasp at their first glimpse of magnificent Zion Valley! After descending to the lush canyon floor, a scenic drive along the north fork of the Virgin River leads to Zion Lodge, the only lodging in the park.

> ### MENU
>
>
> *Baked Brie*
>
> *Southwest Grilled Chicken with Black Bean–Corn Relish*
>
> *Granola Crème Brûlée*

Zion Lodge has a spectacular setting in the valley and is nestled at the base of a towering Navajo sandstone cliff that is part of the canyon's massive east wall. The original lodge and nearby cabins were designed by architect Gilbert Stanley Underwood during the mid-1920s and built in a rustic style with massive sandstone pillars and dramatic wood beams and rafters. Tragically, the main lodge burned to the ground in 1966, but it was rebuilt that same year in just one hundred days. In an effort to maintain service, this rapid reconstruction sacrificed Underwood's classic design and the building's historic appearance. Underwood's original Western-style cabins, however, still remain as part of his architectural legacy at Zion, and in 1990 restoration work was completed that brought back some of the main lodge's original rustic character.

Today, Zion Lodge includes a lobby, an auditorium, a gift shop, a café, and an upstairs dining room. Guests stay year-round in cozy cabins and comfortable rooms and suites with private patios and balconies in two large buildings near the main lodge. The forty rustic cabins near the lodge were restored in 1998 and have pine-plank walls, gas-log fireplaces, and private porches.

Just-arrived visitors can hop on and off Zion's complimentary "in the park" shuttle bus to get a quick orientation and to enjoy some casual sightseeing. A hikers' paradise, the park has trails for adventurous explorers and casual nature-watchers. Lower Emerald Pool is an easy walk to a waterfall; Weeping Rock trail passes a grotto with dripping springs and

"hanging gardens"; and the shady paved Riverside Walk follows the beautiful Virgin River. One of the most popular hiking trails is the multi-day, thirteen-mile West Rim Trail. Those who are in good shape and who aren't afraid of heights enjoy hiking to Hidden Canyon, a steep climb to the mouth of a canyon with pink sands and maidenhair ferns. Angels Landing Trail is a strenuous hike that climbs the famous Walter's Wiggles and has spectacular canyon views. Zion is a wonderful place for wildflower walks in spring and brilliant leaf color in autumn. Photography, bird-watching, and bicycling are also popular activities. Park rangers give guided nature walks and campfire talks, as well as evening lectures at Zion Lodge. Guests enjoy gathering on the lodge's huge front lawn with its 100-foot-tall cottonwood to simply gaze at the stars and drink in the tranquility.

After a day of exploring, visitors look forward to hearty dinners in the spacious Red Rock Grill dining room, which serves breakfast, lunch, and dinner every day. The wood-paneled room has large windows that overlook the canyon, and there is a lovely deck for outdoor dining during fine weather. Chef Jim Fendrick's generous menus offer traditional American cooking and regional Southwestern dishes. Chef Jim Fendrick created the following recipes and presented them to Menus and Music.

Zion Lodge provides comfort year-round in the midst of a beloved and immensely beautiful national park.

ZION LODGE

ZION NATIONAL PARK

UTAH

At Zion National Park, visitors are entranced by a landscape that is both grand and intimate. Throughout the park are colossal stone monuments in shades of vermilion and ochre that tower above visitors, while wildflowers, flowing streams, and gentle birdsong create a delicate counterpoint to the rocky giants.

The park is a geological wonderland, where rivers and streams have cut layers of stone to create sculpted canyons and soaring cliffs. Erosion continues today as the seemingly gentle Virgin River carries away more than one million tons of debris every year. Groves of box elder, willow, and cottonwood trees create a lush riparian landscape. The trees are especially beautiful against the massive stones and cliffs that rise as much as four thousand feet above the canyon floor.

Zion was first brought to national attention when artist Frederick S. Dellenbaugh spent a summer painting the region, then exhibited his paintings at the 1904 St. Louis World's Fair. Zion Canyon, along with many of its rock monuments, was named by Mormon pioneers who came to southern Utah in the late 1840s. When the great Western explorer John Wesley Powell came through the area in 1872, he mistakenly thought the main canyon was called Mukuntuweap by the Paiute tribe. Mukuntuweap National Monument was created by Congress in 1909 and became Zion National Park in 1919. Today, the 229-square-mile park is one of the most popular tourist destinations in Utah and hosts over 2.5 million annual visitors.

In recent years, car exhaust has threatened to destroy Zion Canyon's plant life and peaceful setting. To counteract this problem, the National Park Service designed a shuttle service that runs from nearby Springdale into the park and along the well-traveled Zion Canyon Scenic Drive. When the shuttle runs from April through October, the drive is not accessible to private vehicles. Zion's highly successful shuttle system is being used as a model for dealing with congestion and pollution within the National Park System.

At the park's main visitor center, guests can speak with National Park Service rangers and pick up maps and trail guides. River Walk is a popular trail along the Virgin River, and Weeping Rock is a short hike to an alcove where cool water trickles down a cliff face, and hanging gardens of maidenhair ferns and wildflowers seem to spring from sheer rock.

The valley floor of Zion Canyon is such an amazing destination that few visitors venture into the rest of the park, where outdoor enthusiasts can hike, camp, and rock climb while being surrounded by miles of uninterrupted wilderness. At the Kolob Canyons visitor center, in the park's northwest corner, permits can be obtained for backcountry visits, and a scenic seven-mile trail leads to Kolob Arch, one of the world's longest natural arches.

From April through November, rangers lead guided hikes, narrate shuttle rides, and give talks and slide shows about geology, wildlife, and history. The Zion Canyon Field Institute offers year-round outdoor classes on topics such as mountain wildflowers and trees, geological history, and nature photography. In service-learning classes, participants can work on projects that benefit the park, including archeological inventory and surveys of mountain lion distribution.

At Zion National Park, visitors enjoy awe-inspiring panoramas, outdoor activities in a majestic setting, and exploring within the sheltering walls of an immense canyon.

BAKED BRIE

This appetizer is good for large parties, as the recipe is easy to double or triple.

8 ounces Brie cheese
2 tablespoons packed brown sugar
1/4 cup chopped almonds, toasted (see Basics)
1 Granny Smith apple, peeled, cored, and thinly sliced for garnish
Lavosh (Armenian cracker bread) or French baguette slices for serving

Preheat the oven to 400°F. Put the Brie in a shallow ramekin. Sprinkle with the brown sugar and bake in the preheated oven for 8 to 12 minutes, or until the sugar melts. Remove from the oven and sprinkle with almonds. Serve warm, garnished with apple slices and accompanied with pieces of lavosh or baguette slices. *Makes 4 servings*

SOUTHWEST GRILLED CHICKEN WITH BLACK BEAN–CORN RELISH

A marinade gives the chicken a fresh citrus taste, and the relish adds color and Southwest flavor. Serve with potato salad.

Juice of 8 limes
Juice of 1 orange
1/4 cup chopped fresh cilantro
1/4 cup olive oil
Salt and freshly ground pepper to taste
4 skinless, boneless chicken breast halves
2 corn tortillas
2 cups Black Bean–Corn Relish (recipe follows)

In a medium bowl, combine the lime juice, orange juice, cilantro, olive oil, salt, and pepper. Add the chicken and let stand at room temperature for 30 to 45 minutes, turning once or twice.

Meanwhile, make the tortilla strips: Preheat the oven to 375°F. Cut each tortilla into 4 wedges. Stack the wedges and cut them into matchsticks. Spread the strips on a baking sheet and bake in the preheated oven for 20 minutes, or until crisp.

Prepare a fire in a charcoal grill or preheat the broiler. Grill the chicken breasts over hot coals or under the broiler for 8 minutes on each side, or until opaque throughout. Arrange a chicken breast on each of 4 plates, top with spoonfuls of warm black bean corn relish, and garnish with tortilla strips. *Makes 4 servings*

BLACK BEAN–CORN RELISH

2 cups fresh or thawed frozen corn kernels (about 2 ears corn)
1 red onion, finely diced
1/2 cup chopped fresh cilantro
One 15-ounce can black beans, drained and rinsed
2 small tomatoes, chopped

1 red bell pepper, roasted, seeded, and chopped (see Basics)
2 green onions, white part only, chopped
Juice of 1/2 lime
Salt and freshly ground pepper to taste

Preheat the oven to 400°F. Spread the corn kernels on a baking sheet and bake in the preheated oven for 20 minutes, stirring occasionally, or until light brown and slightly crisp.

In a medium bowl, combine the corn with all the remaining ingredients. *Makes about 4 cups*

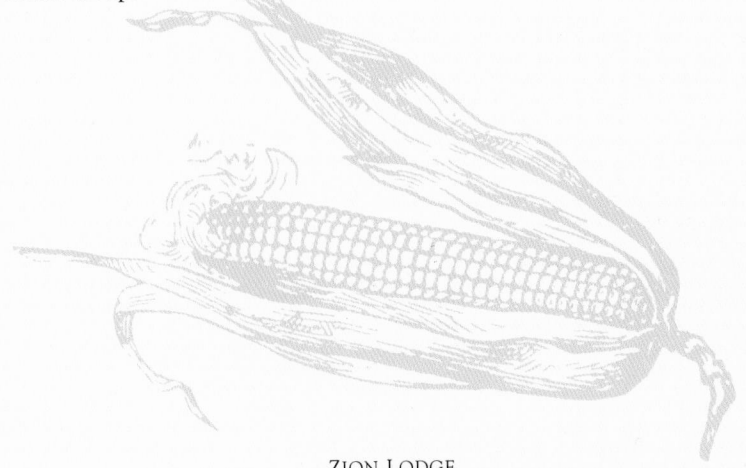

GRANOLA CRÈME BRÛLÉE

A sprinkle of classic Zion Lodge granola adds a crunchy contrast to silky smooth crème brûlée.

4 egg yolks
3 tablespoons sugar
1 cup heavy cream
1 teaspoon vanilla extract

4 tablespoons packed light brown sugar
4 tablespoons Zion Granola (recipe follows)

❧ Preheat oven to 300°F. In a large bowl, whisk the egg yolks and sugar together until thick and pale in color. Whisk in the cream and vanilla. Strain the mixture through a fine-mesh sieve into a large bowl, skimming off any remaining bubbles. Place 4 individual ramekins in a baking dish and pour the custard into the ramekins. Add hot water to the baking pan to come halfway up the sides of the ramekins. Bake in the preheated oven for 50 minutes, or until set on the edges but still trembling in the center. Let cool. Refrigerate for at least 2 hours or up to 48 hours.

❧ Just before serving, preheat the broiler. Place 1 tablespoon of the brown sugar in a small fine-mesh sieve and push the sugar through with the back of a spoon to evenly layer the top of a custard. Repeat with the remaining custards. Place the custards on a baking sheet under the broiler about 2 inches from the heat source and broil until the sugar is melted and crisp, about 1 minute; be careful not to burn. Sprinkle each custard with 1 tablespoon granola. Let cool slightly before serving. *Makes 4 servings*

ZION LODGE GRANOLA

A crunchy garnish for crème brûlée and delicious served at breakfast with yogurt or milk and sliced fresh fruit.

2 cups rolled oats
2 tablespoons chopped almonds
2 tablespoons sesame seeds
2 tablespoons coconut flakes
  (optional)

$3/4$ cup honey
3 tablespoons canola oil
2 tablespoons vanilla extract
$1/2$ cup water
$1/2$ cup raisins

Preheat the oven to 350°F. In a large bowl, combine the oats, almonds, sesame seeds, and optional coconut.

In a small bowl, combine the honey, canola oil, vanilla, and water. Pour into the oat mixture and stir until blended. Spread the granola onto a baking sheet and bake, stirring occasionally, for 20 minutes, or until golden brown. Stir in the raisins. *Makes about 3 cups*

One hardly knows just how to think of it. Never before has such a naked mountain of rock entered our minds. Without a shred of disguise its transcendent form rises pre-eminent. There is almost nothing to compare to it. Niagara has the beauty of energy; the Grand Canyon of immensity; the Yellowstone of singularity; the Yosemite of altitude; the ocean of power; this Great Temple of eternity.

—Frederick S. Dellenbaugh

GRAND CANYON LODGE

GRAND CANYON NATIONAL PARK, ARIZONA

A scenic winding road leads through stately ponderosa pine forests and quaking aspen groves to the stunning Grand Canyon Lodge and Cabins, the only lodging at the Grand Canyon's North Rim. Set at Bright Angel Point at the very edge of the canyon, the lodge is one of the rare places on earth where it's possible to gaze on a desert canyon landscape from a cool alpine forest. Lodge guests can stay in snug historic cabins, enjoy a spectacular dining room that overlooks the canyon, and relax in a remote area away from the crowds.

> **MENU**
>
> Smoked Trout Bruschetta
>
> Pasta Lydia
>
> Desert Blossom

Originally completed in 1928, Grand Canyon Lodge was built as part of the Union Pacific's "Loop Tour," joining the lodges built at Bryce Canyon and Zion to develop tourism in southern Utah. In 1927, the railroad received approval to build a lodge and cabins on the Grand Canyon's North Rim. Designed by Gilbert Stanley Underwood, who was also the architect of Bryce Canyon Lodge and Zion Lodge, the building was constructed of Kaibab limestone and ponderosa logs and almost looked like a natural extension of the canyon walls. An architect of the grand statement, Underwood created a masterpiece. Unfortunately, most of the lodge and several adjacent cabins were destroyed by fire in 1932. With only the stone piers remaining after the blaze, the lodge was rebuilt in 1937 using Underwood's basic plan but eliminating some of the elements that he had brilliantly used to merge building and site.

The reconstructed Grand Canyon Lodge has impressive public spaces that are uniquely Southwestern. The dramatic building has exposed log roof trusses supported by limestone piers between dark stained log walls and wrought iron chandeliers and sconces that use Native American design motifs. A centered entrance leads to the registration desk and lobby. The sun room just off the lobby and the magnificent dining room have framed views of the canyon through huge picture windows. The rooms naturally step down to the canyon rim, and there is an outside terrace with a massive rugged stone fireplace, rocking chairs, and awe-inspiring views out to the horizon. The two wings around the entrance courtyard include a post office, a snack bar, a gift shop, and a Western-style saloon.

It was never intended that guest rooms would be part of the lodge. Instead, overnight guests stay in standard and deluxe log cabins, complete with fireplaces and front porches with relaxing rocking chairs. Built in the 1920s, the cabins are nestled in pine trees and a few of the deluxe cabins have unobstructed views of the canyon.

Guests enjoy paths and trails that originate near the lodge and follow the canyon rim, and for the more adventurous, hiking trails lead to the canyon floor. There are mule trips into the canyon, and National Park Service rangers offer day and evening interpretive programs. Some visitors may even get a glimpse of a California condor, with its amazing nine-foot wing span, or the famed Kaibab squirrel, a squirrel with a white fluffy tail that evolved in the insular environment of this ponderosa pine forest surrounded by desert.

The lodge's immense dining room has some of the most dramatic views of any dining facility in North America. Seven 20-foot tall windows face the canyon, and almost every table in the high-ceilinged room has a panoramic view. The restaurant's generous menu features Southwestern food, but many traditional American and Italian dishes are also included. The restaurant's selection of wines has been carefully chosen. The following recipes were created by Don Botta, who presented them to Menus and Music.

An architectural treasure steeped in history, Grand Canyon Lodge is a spacious, informal place to enjoy a fragile, remote environment.

GRAND CANYON LODGE

SMOKED TROUT BRUSCHETTA

Even smoked boned trout may still retain some small bones, so keep a sharp eye as you mix. This recipe also works well with smoked salmon or smoked chicken.

16 slices Italian bread, sliced $^1/_2$ inch
   thick
$^1/_3$ cup guacamole (see Basics)
$^1/_3$ cup salsa (for homemade,
   see Basics)
16 ounces smoked trout, cut into
   8 slices*
16 fresh cilantro leaves

OPTIONAL GARNISH
2 handfuls baby salad greens
2 or 3 tablespoons salsa
$^1/_2$ cup corn kernels, baked at 350°F
   until crunchy

Prepare a fire in a charcoal grill or preheat the broiler. Toast the bread slices on both sides until golden. Spread 1 teaspoon guacamole on each toasted bread slice. Top with 1 teaspoon salsa and arrange a slice of smoked trout over the salsa. Garnish with a cilantro leaf and arrange on a serving platter. For the optional garnish, arrange a mound of greens topped with salsa and corn kernels in the center of the platter. *Makes 16 bruschetta; serves 4 to 6 as an appetizer*

*Smoked trout is available at some grocery stores and at specialty foods stores.

GRAND CANYON LODGE

PASTA LYDIA

This dish is a favorite of Don Botta, the long-time general manager of Grand Canyon Lodge. The recipe comes from his grandmother and is popular in the stunning Grand Canyon Lodge dining room.

8 small red potatoes, scrubbed and
  halved

10 asparagus spears, trimmed and
  cut into 3-inch lengths

3 tablespoons extra-virgin olive oil

Salt and freshly ground pepper to taste

$1^1/2$ pounds dried bow-tie or
  penne pasta

1 cup pesto (see Basics)

$^1/4$ cup ricotta cheese

2 tablespoons heavy cream

8 cherry tomatoes, halved

$^1/2$ cup pine nuts, toasted (see Basics)

Preheat the oven to 450°F. In a medium bowl, toss the potatoes and asparagus with the olive oil, salt, and pepper. Spread the potatoes and asparagus on a baking sheet and bake in the preheated oven for 7 to 10 minutes, or until tender when pierced with a knife.

In a large pot of salted boiling water, cook the pasta for about 10 minutes, or until al dente; drain.

In a large bowl, combine the pesto, ricotta, and cream and toss with the hot pasta, asparagus, and potatoes. Garnish with the cherry tomatoes and pine nuts and serve at once. *Makes 4 servings*

DESERT BLOSSOM

A crisp, sweet cornucopia filled with sliced fresh fruit.

1 cup ricotta cheese

1/2 cup mascarpone cheese

1/4 cup powdered sugar, sifted

1/4 teaspoon vanilla extract

2 or 3 cups sliced mixed seasonal
  fruits, such as strawberries, mango,
  banana, berries, and pineapple

Juice of 1/2 lime

1/4 cup granulated sugar

2 teaspoons ground cinnamon

Four 6-inch flour tortillas*

4 fresh mint sprigs for garnish

🍃 Preheat the oven to 350°F. Place 4 custard cups or ramekins upside down on a baking sheet.

🍃 In a blender or food processor, add the ricotta, mascarpone, powdered sugar, and vanilla and purée. In a medium bowl, combine the fruit and lime juice.

🍃 In a small bowl, combine the granulated sugar and cinnamon. Using a spray bottle filled with water, mist the tortillas on both sides. Evenly sprinkle the tortillas with cinnamon sugar on both sides. Drape the tortillas over the mugs or cups to form pleated bowls. Bake the tortillas in the preheated oven for 15 to 20 minutes, or until crisp.

🍃 Place a tortilla on its side on each of 4 plates. Spoon an equal portion of the ricotta mixture into the center of each tortilla. Divide the fruit among the cornucopias, letting some spill out onto the plate. Garnish with mint sprigs and serve at once. *Makes 4 servings*

*If the tortillas are larger than 6 inches in diameter, cut them to a 6-inch diameter.

GRAND CANYON NATIONAL PARK

ARIZONA

Probably the world's most spectacular example of the power of erosion, the Grand Canyon's expanse of cliffs and gorges is a geologic museum of epic proportions. It is estimated that the Colorado River has created the canyon over a period of three to six million years and that some of the exposed rock layers at the bottom are almost two billion years old—that is nearly half of the earth's 4.6 billion-year history! Today this World Heritage Site attracts nearly five million visitors annually from around the world.

Native Americans hunted and gathered food in the region for thousands of years before Spaniards of Coronado's expedition discovered the canyon in 1540. When the Santa Fe Trail opened in 1821, American fur trappers, traders, and fortune hunters traveled through the region on their way to California. In 1869, Major John Wesley Powell and his team made a fabled 1,000-mile journey down the Colorado River through the region's previously unexplored canyons. Powell's trip made him a national hero, and his published accounts were so popular that Americans wanted to travel and see the canyon for themselves. In the 1880s, the area attracted prospectors, but it soon became apparent that tourism was more lucrative than mining. In 1919, an act of Congress established 277 miles of the Colorado River and 1,900 square miles surrounding it as Grand Canyon National Park.

The Colorado River divides the park into the North Rim and the South Rim. The inner canyon, which has an average depth of about one mile and an average width of about ten miles, is accessible from either rim. Although the North and South rims are separated by only ten air miles, they are a circuitous 215 miles apart by highway and are distinctly different.

The North Rim is cut off from the rest of Arizona by the canyon itself. This region is visited by only 10 percent of all Grand Canyon visitors, which makes it extraordinary territory for people who enjoy the road less traveled. The only accommodation at the North Rim is the historic Grand Canyon Lodge and Cabins.

The approach to the lodge, through a forest of pines, firs, spruce, and aspen, is especially scenic. Here, the Kaibab Plateau is between 7,800 and 8,800 feet high, and the climate is cooler and wetter than at the South Rim. The North Rim is closed in the snowy months between mid-November and mid-May. At Grand Canyon Lodge, National Park Service rangers offer interpretive day and evening programs, as well as guided hikes throughout the season. Visitors can enjoy guided mule trips into the canyon, as well as trails and paths along the rim that originate near the lodge.

The popular South Rim section of the Grand Canyon is closer to population centers, and its historic buildings, including the flagship El Tovar hotel, were built before the canyon became a national park. Grand Canyon Village is the main center for lodging, meals, and canyon information. The National Park Service offers day and evening programs year-round, and the Grand Canyon Field Institute gives visitors a chance to explore the park for a few days with seasoned guides. In partnership with Xanterra Parks & Resorts, the Institute offers "Learning and Lodging" adventures, and more than ninety classes, including courses on geology, American Indian culture, and desert wildflowers. The famous Grand Canyon mule rides, enjoyed by Presidents, astronauts, and many thousands of others, begin near Bright Angel Lodge. The historic buildings designed by architects Charles Whittlesey and Mary Jane Colter along the South Rim are not to be missed.

Within the Grand Canyon, the Colorado River drops 2,000 feet through 160 major rapids and is considered one of the premier whitewater adventures in North America. Phantom Ranch, a lodge and cabins nestled at the bottom of the Inner Gorge, and campgrounds located within the canyon are accessible only by foot, mule, or raft, and both require reservations well in advance. Although writers, photographers, and storytellers have all tried to describe the Grand Canyon, nothing can really prepare visitors for its awe-inspiring majesty.

BRUCE AIKEN *Horn Creek Rapids* 1998

Leave it as it is. You can not improve on it. The ages have been at work on it,

and man can only mar it. What you can do is to keep it for your children,

your children's children, and for all who come after you, as one of the great

sights which every American if he can travel at all should see.

—President Theodore Roosevelt

EL TOVAR HOTEL

GRAND CANYON NATIONAL PARK, ARIZONA

When the Atchinson, Topeka & Santa Fe Railway completed its spur to the South Rim of the Grand Canyon, the railroad hired architect Charles Whittlesey to create a first-rate hotel for the budding tourist trade. Trained in the Chicago office of Louis Sullivan, Whittlesey created a design that blended European chalet style with the look of a comfortable hunting lodge. His one-hundred-room hotel was built of native stone and Oregon pine, and included chaletlike balconies and terraces, a shingle-covered Victorian turret, and a rustic log-and-plank veranda at the main entrance. When it was completed in 1905, many considered El Tovar the most elegant hotel west of the Mississippi. Named for Don Pedro de Tobar, an officer in the army of the Spanish explorer Coronado, it was part European resort hotel and part rustic log cabin. Uniquely American, the El Tovar provided early visitors with luxurious comfort and a sense of Western adventure, just as it does today.

While Whittlesey was working on El Tovar, architect Mary Jane Colter was hired to design a handful of commercial buildings along the South Rim. Colter, native of Minnesota who studied at the California School of Design, was responsible for designing and decorating at El Tovar, Hopi House, Bright Angel Lodge, Lookout Studio, the Watchtower, and Hermits Rest, as well as Phantom Ranch on the canyon floor. Rather than trying to copy European design styles, her buildings sensitively blend with their settings and draw on the region's cultural traditions.

Grand Canyon National Park was established in 1919, but by then Grand Canyon Village at the South Rim, including the flagship El Tovar hotel, was already built. With the Fred Harvey Company managing the luxurious El Tovar, well-trained Harvey Girl waitresses, famously dressed in black with white aprons, laid out El Tovar silverware, china, and crystal on spotless linen (see page 15). Successful from the start, the luxurious hotel had a

> ## MENU
>
> Black Bean Soup
> with Lime Sour Cream
> and Tortilla Strips
>
> Pan-Seared Salmon Tostadas
> with Fire-Roasted Corn Salsa
>
> Desert Napoleon
> with Raspberry Coulis

music room, a ladies lounge, a solarium, roof gardens, and a formal dining room that overlooked the canyon. The finest fresh foods arrived daily aboard the Santa Fe, and the Harvey Company's own dairy herd provided milk and cheese and a greenhouse ensured fresh flowers for the dining room tables. Over the years, prominent hotel guests have included Theodore Roosevelt, Howard Taft, George Bernard Shaw, Zane Grey, Albert Einstein, and Bill Clinton.

Today, El Tovar has seventy-eight comfortable guest rooms, including twelve themed suites named after Grand Canyon legends, such as the art-filled Zane Grey, Colter, Harvey,

and Whittlesey suites. In the refurbished entrance lobby, dark-stained log-slab walls, heavy beams and rafters, a stone fireplace, and mounted hunting trophies supply the same hunting lodge atmosphere that they did when El Tovar first opened. Guests enjoy breathtaking canyon views along the rim and many get an even better idea of the land's vast beauty by hiking on trails into the canyon. The famous Grand Canyon tradition of riding a sure-footed mule to the canyon floor continues, a trip many thousands have enjoyed. Daily National Park Service programs help explain the canyon's history and geology, and many visitors enjoy motor-coach tours. For those who want to explore the park with informative and entertaining naturalists during the day and stay in comfort at night, "Lodging and Learning" programs are available through the Grand Canyon Field Institute in partnership with Xanterra Parks & Resorts. For music lovers, the Grand Canyon Music Festival presents a series of chamber music concerts in mid-September, and from March to November, Arizona artists display their works on El Tovar's covered back porch.

The renowned El Tovar dining room is a historic and enchanting setting for enjoying fine dining. The casually elegant room has two massive stone fireplaces, an open-truss log ceiling, and four large colorful murals by Bruce Himeche that depict the customs of the Hopi, Apache, Mojave, and Navajo tribes. A side porch facing the canyon has been converted to the Canyon Dining Room, where a Chris Jorgenson painting hangs. The restaurant's seasonal menu offers classic cuisine and regional Southwest dishes that can be paired with selections from the restaurant's well-chosen wine list. Executive chef Joe Nobile created the following recipes and presented them to Menus and Music.

BLACK BEAN SOUP WITH LIME SOUR CREAM AND TORTILLA STRIPS

An outstanding hearty soup that captures the vibrant flavors of the Southwest.

1³/4 cups dried black beans

2 tablespoons bacon fat (rendered from 2 bacon slices) or olive oil

1 onion, diced

1 garlic clove, minced

8 cups chicken stock (see Basics) or canned low-salt chicken broth

1 smoked ham hock

1/3 cup dry sherry

1¹/2 teaspoons chili powder

1 teaspoon ground cumin

2 teaspoons Tabasco sauce

1 tablespoon red wine vinegar

1/2 teaspoon *each* salt and freshly ground pepper

2 corn tortillas

El Tovar Lime Sour Cream (see Basics)

3 green onions, white parts only, thinly sliced

Rinse and pick over the beans. Soak the beans overnight in water to cover by 2 inches. Drain.

In a large saucepan over medium heat, heat the bacon fat or olive oil and sauté the onion for 3 minutes. Add the garlic and sauté for 2 minutes, or until fragrant. Stir in the chicken stock or broth, raise heat to high, and bring to a simmer. Add the ham hock and beans, reduce heat to medium-low, and simmer for 45 to 60 minutes, or until the beans are tender.

Using a large fork, remove the ham hock and transfer it to a plate to cool. Remove the meat from the bone, dice the meat, and add it to the soup. Stir in the sherry, chili powder, cumin, Tabasco, vinegar, salt, and pepper, and simmer for 20 minutes. If you like a smooth soup, transfer the soup to a food processor in batches and purée.

To make the tortilla strips: Preheat the oven to 375°F. Stack the 2 corn tortillas, cut them in half, and stack them again. Cut the stack in half and stack again. Cut the tortillas into matchsticks. Spread the strips on a baking sheet and bake in the preheated oven for 20 minutes, or until crisp.

Ladle the soup into bowls and top with a dollop of lime sour cream. If you wish, use a knife to make decorative sour cream lines in the soup. Sprinkle with green onions and tortilla strips; serve hot. *Makes 6 to 8 servings*

PAN-SEARED SALMON TOSTADAS
WITH FIRE-ROASTED CORN SALSA

At the El Tovar dining room, chef Joe Nobile uses blue corn and red corn tortillas in his delicious signature dish.

Eight 6-inch corn tortillas
2 large handfuls baby salad greens

CHILI OLIVE OIL
1/2 ancho chili*
1/3 cup olive oil
1/2 teaspoon Tabasco sauce

2 tablespoons olive oil or canola oil
4 salmon fillets, pin bones removed
Chile-Lime Rice (recipe follows)
Lime Sour Cream (see Basics)
Fire-Roasted Corn Salsa
  (recipe follows)

🌿 Preheat the oven to 375°F. Spread the tortillas on baking sheets and bake in the preheated oven for 20 minutes, or until crisp.

🌿 To make the chili olive oil: In a small bowl, soak the ancho chili half in hot water for 20 minutes. In a food processor, combine the chili, olive oil, and Tabasco and purée.

🌿 In a medium bowl, toss the salad greens with chili olive oil until the leaves are thoroughly coated.

🌿 In a large frying pan over medium-high heat, heat the olive or canola oil and sauté the salmon for 4 minutes on each side, or until golden brown on the outside and still barely translucent in the center.

🌿 Place a small scoop of chili-lime rice at the top of each of 4 plates. Place a tortilla at 4 and 8 o'clock and top each tortilla with the salad greens. Arrange a salmon fillet over the greens and top with corn salsa and a dollop of lime sour cream. *Makes 4 servings*

*Ancho chilies are available in Latino markets and some grocery stores.

CHILI-LIME RICE

2 tablespoons olive oil
1/2 onion, minced
1 garlic clove, minced
2 tablespoons tomato paste
Juice of 2 limes

3 cups cooked white rice at room
   temperature
2 teaspoons chili powder
1 tablespoon chopped fresh cilantro
Salt and freshly ground pepper to taste

🌿 In a large frying pan over medium heat, heat the olive oil and sauté the onion for 3 minutes. Add the garlic and sauté for 3 minutes, or until golden. Stir in the tomato paste and cook until it browns. Add the lime juice and stir in the cooked rice, chili powder, and cilantro. Season with salt and pepper. Serve warm. *Makes about 3 cups*

FIRE-ROASTED CORN SALSA

Prepare the salsa at least 1 hour before you plan to serve it so the flavors have a chance to blend.

3 ears fresh corn
1/3 cup canola oil or olive oil
1/2 jalapeno chili, seeded and finely
   diced
1/4 *each* green and red bell pepper,
   seeded, deribbed, and finely diced

2 tablespoons chopped fresh cilantro
1/2 small red onion, finely diced
Salt and freshly ground pepper to taste
1 tomato, diced
1/2 cup V-8 juice

🌿 Prepare a fire in a charcoal grill or preheat a broiler. Rub each ear of corn with canola or olive oil and grill or broil, turning frequently, until the kernels are slightly charred. Remove and let cool. Using a sharp knife, remove the kernels from the cobs. In a medium bowl, combine the corn and all the remaining salsa ingredients and mix thoroughly. Let stand at room temperature for 1 hour, stirring occasionally. *Makes 4 servings*

DESERT NAPOLEON WITH RASPBERRY COULIS

At the El Tovar dining room, these Napoleons are served surrounded with raspberry coulis and vanilla sauce or blue curaçao.

Four 6-inch flour tortillas, cut into triangles
$^1/_2$ cup sugar mixed with $^1/_4$ cup ground cinnamon
$1^1/_2$ cups heavy cream
3 kiwis, peeled and thinly sliced

1 pint fresh strawberries, hulled and quartered
1 pint fresh blueberries
2 bananas, thinly sliced
4 sprigs fresh mint
Raspberry Coulis (recipe follows)
Vanilla Sauce (see Basics)

Preheat the oven to 350°F. Spread the tortillas on a baking sheet and bake for 15 to 20 minutes, or until crisp. Remove from the oven and generously sprinkle with the cinnamon sugar.

In a deep bowl, beat the cream until soft peaks form. Place a dollop of whipped cream in the center of each plate and top with a cinnamon tortilla triangle. Place 2 tablespoons of each of the fruits on top of each tortilla. Top with a dollop of whipped cream. Repeat twice. Top with a fourth triangle. Garnish with a dollop of whipped cream, more fruit, and a mint sprig. Drizzle with raspberry coulis and vanilla sauce and serve immediately. *Makes 4 servings*

Mountains of music well in the rivers, hills of music billow in the creeks,

and meadows of music murmur in the rills that ripple over the rocks,

while other melodies are heard in the gorges of the lateral canyons.

The Grand Canyon is a land of song.

—John Wesley Powell

RASPBERRY COULIS

1 cup fresh or thawed frozen raspberries

2 tablespoons sugar

2 teaspoons fresh orange juice

1 teaspoon fresh lemon juice

2 teaspoons cornstarch mixed with
2 teaspoons cold water

In a food processor, combine the raspberries, sugar, orange juice, and lemon juice and purée. Transfer to a medium saucepan and bring to a boil over medium-high heat. Stir in the cornstarch mixture until dissolved. Return to a boil, reduce heat to medium-low, and simmer for 5 minutes, or until thickened. Strain through a fine-mesh sieve into a bowl. Let cool and refrigerate until chilled. *Makes about 1 cup*

TIMBERLINE LODGE
MT. HOOD, OREGON

Timberline is a mountain lodge masterpiece, a beloved ski resort famous for its Northwest cuisine, and a living museum of arts and crafts. Solidly planted just above the timberline of snow-capped Mt. Hood, Oregon's highest peak, the dramatic hexagonal building is a grand example of Cascadian architecture. It was constructed and furnished entirely by hand during the Great Depression and stands as a tribute to the spirit of the Pacific Northwest. Almost two million skiers, hikers, and nature lovers from around the world visit here every year.

Timberline Lodge was built by hundreds of Works Progress Administration (WPA) workers in 1936 and 1937. The project provided life sustaining jobs for more than 500 men and women, many over the age of fifty-five and all in desperate need of employment. Although the work began in the spring with fourteen feet of snow on the ground, incredibly the building was completed in just fifteen months. The design is derived from European chateaux and alpine chalet architecture and is imbued with the spirit of several National Park structures built by Gilbert Stanley Underwood, the consulting architect of the project.

The coordination of furnishings and decorations was supervised by Margery Hoffman Smith, a Portland decorator, who convinced the Federal Arts Project to commission original oil paintings, wood reliefs, incised linoleum panels, mosaics, and stained glass. Whenever possible, recycled materials were used, including utility poles for carved newel posts, old railroad tracks for fireplace andirons, and uniforms from the Civilian Conservation Corps that were cut into strips and hooked into rugs. At one point, there were more than 200 women hand weaving Oregon wool, yarn, and flax for upholstery, bedspreads, and draperies. When the project was complete, many workers were moved to tears because they knew they had created something more important than just a building. Timberline houses

MENU

Astoria Clam Chowder

Pan-Seared Breast of
Chicken with Chanterelle,
Shiitake, and Sherry Sauce

Marionberry-Ginger
Crisp with Kirsch-Hazelnut
Streusel

a permanent catalogued exhibition of American design, painting, and craftwork of the 1930s. In 1975, the Friends of Timberline, a nonprofit organization, was established for the purpose of conserving and restoring the lodge rooms and furnishings.

Timberline was closed during World War II, and by the 1950s it was in a sad state of disrepair. Richard L. Kohnstamm fell in love with the lodge and made it his personal crusade to restore it and bring it back to life. In 1955, Kohnstamm established a lease with the U.S. Forest Service and began to repair major systems and to restore the lodge interior and furnishings. Today, Kohnstamm's RLK Company has a long-term operating lease for the lodge.

Lodge guests can enjoy year-round skiing, snowboarding, and cross-country skiing. Ski and snowboarding lessons are available for beginners, and most of the mountain is ideal for intermediate level skiers. Summer activities include skiing, hiking, mountain biking, horseback riding, and climbing. Nearby is a championship golf course, white-water rafting, fishing, and sailboarding. Timberline has an outdoor swimming pool and whirl-pool as well as an indoor sauna. Every October, the main lounge becomes a live concert venue during the popular Acoustic Music Series.

After a day of skiing or hiking, guests can retreat to cozy guest rooms with handmade furnishings and original wildflower watercolors. In addition, there are ten chalet bunk rooms with shared restrooms for groups and families. The main lounge serves as the lodge "living room" and the six-sided, fifty-five-foot-tall room has a huge stone chimney with three warming fireplaces.

Just off the Main Lounge, the Cascade Dining Room entrance gate is a marvel of wrought iron, with a design that includes animal heads, Indian symbols, pinecones, and a door handle forged in the shape of a rattlesnake. The dining room is built entirely of fir, including the heavy dining room chairs with hand-carved backs in the shape of the "Timberline Lodge arch" found throughout the building. There is a charming Erick Lamade carving of a woodland scene over the stone fireplace, and white tablecloths, candles, and flowers create a romantic atmosphere in the evening. Executive chef Leif Benson's award-winning menus showcase Northwest cuisine, with accents from around the world. A lead-ing pioneer of Northwest cuisine, he uses fresh seasonal foods of the region, and his hearty dishes are served in generous portions suitable for a recreational area. Benson's travels to Asia and his interest in Native American cuisine add exciting influences to the menu. The restaurant's extensive wine list features Oregon and Washington wines, as well as microbrewed ales from the Mt. Hood Brewing Company. Chef Benson created the follow-ing recipes for Menus and Music.

Timberline Lodge's strong character, down-to-earth simplicity, and artistic celebra-tion of the Northwest region set it apart. The lodge has endeared itself to the residents of the Pacific Northwest and to all those who have celebrated in this place of unique beauty and dignity.

DARREL AUSTIN *The Musicians* 1936

CHARLES HEANEY *Mountain* 1937

Here I am on the slopes of Mt. Hood, where I've always wanted to come.

I'm here to dedicate a monument to the skill and faithful performance of workers

on the rolls of the Works Progress Administration—unique in all America.

—Franklin Delano Roosevelt

ASTORIA CLAM CHOWDER

At Timberline Lodge, chef Leif Benson's classic Northwest clam chowder often includes geoduck or razor clams. Serve with crusty French bread, sweet butter, and a glass of chilled Chardonnay.

4 pounds clams, scrubbed and rinsed

2 bacon slices, diced

2 tablespoons unsalted butter

1 onion, diced

1 cup diced celery

1 red bell pepper, seeded, deribbed, and finely diced

1 teaspoon minced fresh thyme

$1/2$ cup all-purpose flour

4 cups milk

4 to 6 unpeeled small red new potatoes, diced

1 teaspoon salt

$1/4$ teaspoon ground white pepper

In a large saucepan, bring 2 cups water to a boil over medium-high heat. Add the clams, cover, and cook until all the clams open, about 5 minutes. Discard any clams that do not open. Remove the meat from the shells, chop, and set aside. Strain the broth through a fine-mesh sieve and reserve.

In a large saucepan over medium heat, fry the bacon until crisp. Add the butter to the pan and sauté the onion for 3 minutes, or until translucent. Add the celery, bell pepper, and thyme and sauté for 5 minutes, or until the bell pepper is soft. Stir in the flour and cook for 3 minutes, stirring constantly.

In a medium saucepan, combine the milk, clams, reserved clam broth, and potatoes. Bring to a boil over medium-high heat. Gradually pour the milk mixture into the saucepan with the vegetables, stirring constantly until blended. Season with salt and pepper. Return the soup to a boil, reduce heat to medium-low, and simmer for 30 minutes, or until the potatoes are soft. If the soup becomes too thick, add more milk. *Makes 6 to 8 servings*

PAN-SEARED BREAST OF CHICKEN WITH CHANTERELLE, SHIITAKE, AND SHERRY SAUCE

With their ruffled tops and distinctive woodsy flavor, chanterelles are one of the most delicious of the wild Northwest mushrooms.

6 boneless, skinless chicken breast halves
Salt and freshly ground pepper to taste
Olive oil for brushing

CHANTERELLE, SHIITAKE, AND SHERRY SAUCE

12 ounces mixed chanterelle and stemmed shiitake mushrooms
2 tablespoons unsalted butter
$1/2$ small onion, minced
1 garlic clove, minced
1 teaspoon minced fresh marjoram
Salt and freshly ground pepper to taste
$1/2$ cup dry sherry
1 cup heavy cream or half-and-half

🌿 Sprinkle both sides of the chicken breasts with salt and pepper. Heat a grill pan over medium-high heat, brush the grids with olive oil, and cook the chicken for 5 to 6 minutes on each side, or until golden on the outside and the juices run clear when pierced at the thickest point.

🌿 To make the sauce: Quickly rinse the mushrooms or wipe them clean. Pat dry with paper towels and halve or slice the mushrooms if large.

🌿 In a large frying pan, melt the butter and sauté the onion for 3 minutes. Add the garlic and sauté for 2 minutes; do not let the garlic brown. Add the mushrooms, increase heat to medium-high, and sauté for 5 minutes, or until tender. Stir in the marjoram, salt, and pepper. Transfer the mushrooms to a plate and keep warm.

🌿 Return the frying pan to medium-high heat, add the sherry, and stir to scrape up any browned bits from the bottom of the pan. Add the cream or half-and-half and cook until the liquid is reduced by one-third. Season with salt and pepper. Set aside and keep warm.

🌿 To serve, thinly slice the chicken and fan out the slices on each of 4 warmed plates. Top with the mushrooms, spoon the sauce over, and serve immediately.
Makes 6 servings

MARIONBERRY-GINGER CRISP
WITH KIRSCH-HAZELNUT STREUSEL

Ginger and a superb streusel topping update this old-fashioned dessert and complement the fabulous flavor of marionberries. Serve with your favorite ice cream.

6 cups fresh or frozen marionberries*

5 tablespoons sugar

1 tablespoon cornstarch

Juice and grated zest of 1 lemon
 (see Basics)

1 tablespoon minced peeled
 fresh ginger

1 teaspoon freshly ground black
 pepper

KIRSCH-HAZELNUT STREUSEL

4 tablespoons cold unsalted butter,
 cut into small pieces

5 tablespoons sugar

$1/2$ cup all-purpose flour

2 tablespoons ground toasted skinned
 hazelnuts (see Basics)

1 tablespoon kirsch**

$3/4$ cup hazelnuts, toasted, skinned,
 and chopped (see Basics)

Preheat the oven to 350°F. In a medium saucepan, bring the berries and sugar to a boil over medium-high heat. In a small bowl, combine the cornstarch and lemon juice and stir to make a paste. Stir the cornstarch mixture into the berries and cook, stirring occasionally, until thickened. Add the ginger, pepper, and lemon zest. Reduce heat and simmer for 2 minutes. Set aside.

To make the streusel: In a food processor, combine all the ingredients and pulse just until crumbly, about 15 seconds.

Spoon the marionberry mixture into 6 individual ovenproof ramekins. Top evenly with streusel and chopped hazelnuts. Bake in the preheated oven for 30 minutes, or until the streusel is golden brown and the berries are bubbling.
Makes 6 servings

*A cultivated type of blackberry, marionberries are an important Northwest crop. Blackberries may be substituted.

**Kirsch is cherry brandy.

HOWARD S. SEWALL *Timberline Lodge* c. 1937

THE AHWAHNEE HOTEL

Yosemite National Park, California

Set in a meadow on the Yosemite Valley floor and surrounded by the natural beauty that has inspired so many, the grand Ahwahnee Hotel offers luxurious hospitality in a lodge that has been famous since the day it opened in 1927. The beloved building is architect Gilbert Stanley Underwood's most stunning example of rustic architecture in a national park.

Underwood's legendary lodge is built on a grand scale and faced with rough-cut granite and concrete stained to look like redwood siding and milled timbers. Its walls and green slate roofs blend the structure with the surrounding forest and its granite cliff

MENU

*Beer-Braised Mussels
with Tomato and Basil*

*Pork Chops
with Appaloosa Bean Chili
and Fried Onion Rings*

Ahwahnee Boysenberry Pie

backdrop, the Royal Arches. Throughout the Ahwahnee's public rooms, a priceless collection of paintings, photographs, baskets, and rugs is displayed. The spectacular Great Lounge has two enormous stone fireplaces facing each other across the room, and comfortable couches and chairs and a magnificent piano make it inviting. The room's twenty-four-foot-high ceiling has exposed beams with painted Indian motifs, large wrought-iron chandeliers, and floor-to-ceiling windows topped with colorful stained glass panels. Just off the Great Lounge is a light-filled solarium with an indoor pond; the Winter Club Room, with park memorabilia; and the lovely Mural Room (originally the writing room) with a mural by Robert Boardman Howard that depicts the flora and fauna of Yosemite Valley. The hotel has ninety-nine guest rooms in the main building and twenty-four in cozy cottages nearby.

A great time to visit Yosemite is in spring, when the park's spectacular waterfalls explode with wintry runoff. In warmer weather, visitors enjoy hiking, backpacking, fishing, and horseback riding. In Yosemite Valley, there are photography walks, interpretive programs, bicycling, and sightseeing tours. The internationally renowned Yosemite Mountaineering School offers rock-climbing classes and guided climbs. In winter, guests can head up to Badger Pass, a family-oriented ski resort, or visit Curry Village in the Valley, where there is ice skating under the trees and stars. After a day of exhilarating fun, relaxing afternoon tea

is served daily in the Great Lounge of The Ahwahnee. Entertaining board games are available at the front desk, and at night there are educational films and lectures.

The Ahwahnee dining room is often described as one of the most beautiful restaurants in America. Its tall trestle-beamed ceiling, floor-to-ceiling windows framing gorgeous views, and dramatic wrought-iron chandeliers make it romantic and magical. The dinner menu offers traditional American dishes and seasonal California cuisine with Mediterranean and Asian influences. The pianists that perform during dinner have inspired generations of music-lovers. The Bracebridge Dinner is an Ahwahnee holiday tradition that has been popular since its inception in 1927. This three-hour Christmas pageant, based on Washington Irving's *Sketch Book*, combines a fabulous seven-course dinner with music and drama in the grand dining room. Ansel Adams, whose passion for photography and music were almost equal, was the Bracebridge Dinner director for forty-two years, and today Andrea Fulton leads a cast of one hundred to continue the tradition. Each fall, the Vintners' Holidays program introduces guests to wonderful wines and the people who make them, and in January and February renowned chefs give cooking demonstrations during the Chefs' Holidays series. The following recipes were presented to Menus and Music by executive chef James Anile.

The Ahwahnee has greeted presidents, queens, international celebrities, and thousands of guests over the years, who all come to stay in an architectural masterpiece set in the hallowed landscape of Yosemite National Park.

THE AHWAHNEE HOTEL

YOSEMITE NATIONAL PARK
CALIFORNIA

1851, the Mariposa Battalion entered the valley by order of the state of California to end the "Mariposa Indian War."

Word of the spectacular region spread quickly, thanks in part to artists such as Albert Bierstadt. Visitors arrived on foot, horseback, and by stagecoach, and entrepreneurs constructed hotels and residences. John Muir, often called the "father of our national park system," and one of America's most influential naturalists, had an intense love for Yosemite. His struggle against the devastation of the sub-alpine meadows surrounding Yosemite Valley resulted in the creation of Yosemite National Park in 1890. The Sierra Club, formed in 1892 by John Muir and other supporters, continues to work for the preservation of Yosemite and other important natural resources worldwide. Ansel Adams, one of America's foremost photographers, was also an activist with the Sierra Club and worked in Yosemite for many years. The Ansel Adams Gallery in Yosemite Village was once operated by Adams and his wife, and today the popular gallery sponsors instructional photography walks in the park.

Yosemite is home to Half Dome and El Capitan, two of the most spectacular granite rocks towering thousands of feet above the valley floor. Free shuttle buses operate in the valley year-round and in other parts of the park during the summer. There are guided walks, art classes, family programs, and hundreds of free educational programs. Near the landmark Victorian-style Wawona Hotel, the oldest hotel in the park, is the Mariposa grove of giant sequoias, remarkable trees that live for thousands of years and grow hundreds of feet tall. In Yosemite's high country, visitors can enjoy Tuolumne Meadows, the Yosemite Mountaineering School, trails for day hikers and backpackers, and four- and six-day saddle trips. In winter, Badger Pass is a popular destination for skiing.

More than four million people visit Yosemite every year to marvel at its beauty and to enjoy adventures in its beloved landscape. Yosemite is a thrilling place of natural splendor and an American treasure that is truly worth protecting for generations to come.

Set in California's Sierra Nevada mountains and treasured for the grandeur of its towering granite cliffs, giant sequoia groves, and thundering waterfalls, Yosemite is a gem in the national park system. Yosemite was deemed an inalienable public trust by President Abraham Lincoln in 1864, the first time in history that a federal government had set aside scenic lands simply to preserve them for the enjoyment of all people.

About ten million years ago, the Sierra Nevada began to tilt, forming their dramatic eastern slopes and gentler western slopes. The uplift made streams and rivers run more quickly, cutting deep canyons in the land. About one million years ago, glaciers formed in the alpine meadows and proceeded to move down the canyons. The thickness of the ice in Yosemite Valley may have reached 4,000 feet during the glacial period. These ice masses created the U-shaped Yosemite Valley and its scenic vistas.

Native Americans first lived in Yosemite approximately 8,000 years ago. Their culture included caring for their resources, and early visitors were surprised by the well-tended landscape, not realizing that the native inhabitants practiced selective burning. In 1849, gold miners in the Sierra Nevada foothills clashed violently with the native people. In

BEER-BRAISED MUSSELS
WITH TOMATO AND BASIL

Bursting with flavor, this dish makes a delicious first course or a light supper when served with crusty bread and a green salad. Enjoy with an icy cold beer.

6 tablespoons unsalted butter

2 garlic cloves, chopped

1 small shallot, chopped

1 pound mussels, scrubbed and
   debearded

One 12-ounce bottle dark beer or stout,
   such as German bock beer, Guinness
   stout, or Anchor Steam beer

1 tomato, peeled, seeded, and diced

2 tablespoons finely shredded fresh
   basil leaves (see Basics)

Dash *each* of Tabasco and
   Worcestershire sauce

Salt and freshly ground pepper to taste

4 slices crusty French bread, toasted

In a large frying pan, melt 2 tablespoons of the butter over medium-high heat. Add the garlic, shallot, and mussels and sauté for 1 minute. Add the beer, cover, and cook for 2 minutes. Stir in the tomato, basil, Tabasco, and Worcestershire. Discard any mussels that do not open. Using a slotted spoon, transfer the mussels to a bowl and cover to keep warm. Increase heat to high and cook the braising liquid until reduced by half. Season with salt and pepper. Divide the mussels among 4 bowls, ladle in some of the braising liquid, and top with a slice of toasted bread; serve immediately. *Makes 4 first-course servings*

On entering The Ahwahnee, one is conscious of calm and complete beauty echoing the mood of majesty and peace that is the essential quality of Yosemite . . .

—Ansel Adams

PORK CHOPS WITH APPALOOSA BEAN CHILI AND FRIED ONION RINGS

MARINADE

2 cups olive oil

1/4 cup each minced shallots and garlic

1 sprig fresh rosemary

2 arbol chilies, chopped

1 tablespoon black peppercorns

1/4 cup Jim Beam whiskey

4 pork loin chops, about 1 inch thick

SPICE RUB

1 tablespoon granulated garlic

1 tablespoon granulated onion

1 teaspoon *each* cayenne pepper and
  ground black pepper

2 tablespoons salt

2 tablespoons Hungarian paprika

1 tablespoon packed brown sugar

1 tablespoon chili powder

ONION RINGS

1 1/2 cups all-purpose flour

1/4 cup sweet Hungarian paprika

1 tablespoon each garlic powder,
  onion powder, cayenne pepper, salt,
  and pepper

2 onions, sliced into thin rings

2 cups peanut oil or canola oil

Appaloosa Bean Chili (recipe follows)

In a bowl just large enough to hold the pork chops, combine all the marinade ingredients. Add the pork chops and marinate at room temperature for 1 to 2 hours, turning occasionally. In a small bowl, combine all the spice rub ingredients.

Preheat the oven to 350°F. Prepare a fire in a charcoal grill or preheat a broiler. Remove the chops from the marinade and pat dry with paper towels. Rub them with the spice rub. Grill or broil the pork chops for 2 minutes on each side, or until browned. Transfer the chops to a baking dish and bake in the preheated oven for 45 minutes.

To make the onion rings: In a large bowl, combine the flour and spices. Add the onions and toss until dredged. In a Dutch oven or deep-fat fryer, heat the oil until an onion dropped into the fat sizzles. Add the onion rings in small batches and cook for 3 minutes, or until golden brown. Using a slotted spoon, transfer to paper towels.

To serve, spoon a mound of chili on each of 4 warmed plates and top with a pork chop. Top each chop with onion rings and serve at once. *Makes 4 servings*

THE AHWAHNEE HOTEL

THOMAS HILL *Scene of Yosemite: Bridalveil Fall* c. 1871 California Historical Society

APPALOOSA BEAN CHILI

A fabulous, hearty chili. Appaloosa beans are spotted beans named after the Appaloosa horse. If they are unavailable, substitute pinto beans.

2 tablespoons bacon fat or olive oil
4 garlic cloves, minced
1 onion, finely diced
2 tablespoons cumin seeds, toasted
  and ground
2 tablespoons coriander seeds, toasted
  and ground
1 serrano chili, seeded and chopped
2 cups dried appaloosa beans or pinto
  beans, soaked overnight in cold
  water and drained

One 12-ounce bottle of beer
4 cups chicken stock (see Basics) or
  canned low-salt chicken broth
1 smoked ham hock
2 teaspoons salt
2 teaspoons ancho chili purée
  (see Basics)
1/2 bunch cilantro, steeped in 1 cup
  boiling water for 10 minutes
Juice of 2 limes

In a large saucepan over medium heat, melt the bacon fat or heat the oil and sauté the garlic until golden, about 4 minutes. Add the onion and sauté for 3 minutes. Stir in the cumin and coriander and sauté for 2 minutes, or until the spices are fragrant. Add the serrano chili, beans, and beer, stirring to scrape up any browned bits from the bottom of the pan. Cook, stirring occasionally, until the beer reduces by two-thirds. Add the stock or broth, ham hock, and ancho purée and bring to a boil, skimming off any foam that rises to the surface. Reduce heat to medium-low and simmer for 1 hour, or until the beans are tender.

Remove the ham hock and let cool. Cut the meat away from the bone and dice. Transfer about one-third of the bean mixture to a food processor and purée. Put the cilantro in a medium bowl and pour 1 cup boiling water over; set aside and let steep for 10 minutes. Discard the cilantro and pour the cilantro-infused water into the chili. Stir in the diced ham, puréed beans, and salt. Reheat the chili. Add the lime juice. Taste and adjust the seasoning. Serve hot. *Makes 6 to 8 servings*

AHWAHNEE BOYSENBERRY PIE

A signature dessert in the grand dining room of the Ahwahnee. This recipe also works well with fresh blackberries and is especially delicious served with vanilla ice cream.

PASTRY

2 cups all-purpose flour

1/2 teaspoon salt

3 tablespoons sugar

1 cup (2 sticks) cold unsalted butter, cut into small pieces

1/3 cup cold water

1 egg, beaten with 1 tablespoon water

FILLING

6 cups fresh or frozen boysenberries

1/2 cup sugar

3 tablespoons instant tapioca

Pinch of salt

To make the pastry: In a food processor, combine the flour, salt, sugar, and butter. Process until the mixture resembles coarse crumbs, about 15 seconds. With the machine running, add the water and process until the mixture begins to form a ball, about 20 seconds. Flatten the dough into 2 disks, cover with plastic wrap, and refrigerate for at least 1 hour.

Preheat the oven to 350°F. On a lightly floured surface, roll out one of the disks to a 12-inch round. Fit into a 10-inch pie pan and trim the edges. Bake in the preheated oven for 5 minutes.

In a medium saucepan, cook the boysenberries over low heat for 5 minutes. In a small bowl, stir the sugar, tapioca, and salt together. Stir the sugar mixture into the berries and cook, stirring frequently, for 5 minutes, or until thickened. Remove from the heat and set aside.

On a lightly floured surface, roll out the top crust. Pour the berry filling into the pie shell. Brush the rim of the filled pie shell with the egg mixture. Place the top crust over the pie, trim, and press with a fork all around to seal the edges. Brush the top crust with the egg mixture and cut 4 slits in the crust. Bake in the preheated oven for 50 to 60 minutes, or until the crust is golden brown. Remove from the oven and let cool before serving. *Makes one 10-inch pie*

THE AHWAHNEE HOTEL

FURNACE CREEK INN

DEATH VALLEY NATIONAL PARK, CALIFORNIA

A magnificent oasis resort in a remote and surprising desert, the Furnace Creek Inn is a glamorous getaway that attracts visitors worldwide. Three natural springs converge above the inn, feeding the naturally warm swimming pool and providing water for lush lawns and the palm garden. Temperatures at Furnace Creek are quite comfortable from October through May, ranging from the high 70s to the low 80s. During the summer, however, it is typically 100°F and often approaches 120°F! Located just two hours from Las Vegas, this AAA four-diamond property is surrounded by 3,000 square miles of arid desert, making the inn a true hideaway.

> **MENU**
>
> *Crisp Cactus Appetizers*
>
> *Stuffed Mojave Chicken*
>
> *Chocolate Truffles*

The Furnace Creek Inn opened in 1927 as a private corporate retreat for guests of the Pacific Coast Borax Company. Los Angeles architect Albert Martin designed the mission-style structure and set it into a low ridge overlooking Furnace Creek Wash. The inn's adobe bricks were handmade on site by Paiute and Shoshone laborers, and stonemason Steve Esteves laid the artistic stonework. In the late 1920s, almost 1,500 date and fan palms were planted on more than 33 acres at Furnace Creek. With the addition of a 9-hole golf course and the swimming pool, the inn was completed in 1935.

Today an airstrip makes the Furnace Creek Inn accessible by private plane, and many guests come to enjoy the eighteen-hole golf course designed by Perry Dye. At 214 feet below sea level, this is the lowest grass course in the world, and golfers are challenged by a distinct difference in the way the ball responds compared with above-sea-level courses.

Death Valley's awe-inspiring mountains and canyons, as well as its crystal-clear air that makes colors more vivid, have attracted many filmmakers. More than forty films and television shows have used the area as a backdrop, including *Star Wars, Spartacus,* and *Death Valley Days,* which was hosted by Ronald Reagan. Prominent guests have included such movie stars as Anthony Quinn, Dennis Hopper, and Peter Fonda.

Traditionally, guests enjoy evenings by the inn's seventy-foot outdoor swimming pool. They can also play a game of tennis on one of four lighted courts, have a massage, stargaze,

or take in an early-morning walk, jog, or hike. Activities farther afield include motoring down Artist's Drive, a one-way road that meanders through multi-hued washes and rock formations, or visiting Scotty's Castle, an amazing compound built in the 1920s that replicates a Spanish manor. Close by are the Harmony Borax Works and the Borax Museum, with its antique stagecoaches, mining tools, and a steam locomotive. Just outside park boundaries is the fancifully painted Amargosa Opera House, where Marta Beckett has performed ballet pantomimes for more than thirty years.

The Furnace Creek Inn maintains an atmosphere of classic 1930s elegance, and the resort's sixty-six-rooms and two suites are decorated in a style that recalls the inn's rich history. The nearby Furnace Creek Ranch offers 224 simple family-style accommodations. The Furnace Creek Inn & Ranch Resort is managed by Cal and Toni Jepson.

The Inn dining room is an elegant and historic setting for fine dining. The quiet room is perfect for conversation and has stunning views of the Panamint Mountains. Crisp white tablecloths, candlelight, cobalt blue goblets, and music from the Big Band era set the mood. The menu offers classic, Southwestern, and Pacific-Rim cuisine, along with a carefully chosen list of California varietal wines. A lavish Sunday brunch is served in season. Chef Michelle Hanson created the following recipes for Menus and Music.

DEATH VALLEY NATIONAL PARK

CALIFORNIA

Death Valley, the largest national park in the continental United States, was established by an act of Congress in 1994. It encompasses 3.3 million acres of stunning desert scenery, 95 percent of which is undisturbed wilderness. Although temperatures in the valley range from the mid-60s to low 90s between October and March, it is one of the hottest places on earth during the summer, with temperatures of over 120°F quite common. Despite the heat, superbly adapted desert wildlife and more than one thousand species of plants live within the park, including some with roots that go down more than fifty feet!

A land of contrasts and extremes, the park has some of the most dramatic landscapes in the United States. For instance, snow-covered Telescope Mountain in the park's Panamint Mountain Range has an elevation of 11,049 feet, yet it is only fifteen miles from Badwater Basin, the lowest point in the Western Hemisphere. Badwater, 282 feet below sea level, is a salt-crusted pool of water with four to five times the salt content of the ocean. The park's Ubehebe Crater is one of the world's largest volcanic-explosion pits. Over two thousand years ago, water flashed to steam upon hitting hot underlying rock, and this violent release of steam-powered energy created a crater that is a half mile across and more than 700 feet deep. Visitors are amazed by the Devil's Golf Course, a vast expanse of rock salt that has been eroded by wind and rain into jagged spires. A shallow lake that dried up around 2,000 years ago, the "golf course's" salt is three to five feet deep. The salt floor of Death Valley can even creak on hot days as it expands in the shimmering heat. At the Racetrack, boulders are sometimes blown by winter winds across frozen mud, leaving behind long and seemingly mysterious tracks.

The valley was originally inhabited by Panamint Indians of the Soshone Nation and their predecessors. In 1849, a group of American pioneers known as the Jayhawkers discovered the valley while traveling from Utah to the California Gold Rush by way of a shortcut through the desert basin. They became trapped for weeks near Badwater Basin. After finally finding their way out of the valley, a departing member of the party looked back and muttered a heartfelt "Good-bye, death valley." In the 1880s, the discovery of borax, the "white gold of the desert," led to a profitable mining period. Harmony Borax Works was built in 1882, and the company's legendary twenty-mule teams pulled sixteen-foot-long wagons of borax more than 165 miles to the nearest railroad stop in Mojave.

Today, visitors to the park can stop at the Furnace Creek visitor center, which includes a museum and a bookstore, and plan their stay with National Park Service rangers. The park's Zabriskie Point, which overlooks colorful, undulating badlands, was the site of the film *Zabriskie Point* by Antonioni (1969). The gorgeous multicolored Artist's Drive Formation drapes across the face of the Black Mountains, and its pink, green, purple, and black rocks are especially photogenic in late-afternoon light. After particularly "wet" springs, great masses of wildflowers cover the desert with riotous colors. Death Valley's clear air can make colors even more vivid, and there are astonishing views of the constellations in the night skies.

Over the years, Death Valley's extreme isolation has attracted a cast of colorful characters, including Walter Scott, better known as "Death Valley Scotty." Once a performer in Buffalo Bill Cody's Wild West Show, Scotty built an elaborate Spanish-style mansion during the 1920s for his friend Albert Johnson, a Chicago millionaire. The complex of more than eight buildings is about fifty-five miles north of Furnace Creek and includes artisan-made tile work, furniture, and interior decorations.

More than one million people visit Death Valley every year to experience the park's clean air, pleasant winter climate, vast open spaces, and overwhelming silence. It may take visitors a few days to attune their senses to the subtle palette of the landscape, but the rare, rugged, and desolate beauty of Death Valley is like nothing else on earth and is not to be missed.

CRISP CACTUS APPETIZERS

Spicy deep-fried cactus slices to serve with salsa, guacamole, or jalapeno jelly for dipping. Delicious with dry sherry or margaritas.

One 16-ounce jar nopalitos*
1 cup all-purpose flour
1 teaspoon *each* pure chile powder,
    ground cumin, paprika, salt, and
    freshly ground pepper

Peanut or canola oil for deep-frying
Salt to taste
Salsa (for homemade, see Basics),
    guacamole (see Basics), or jalapeno
    jelly for serving

Rinse the nopalitos under cold running water. Squeeze dry, then pat dry with paper towels. In a medium bowl, combine the flour and spices. Stir to blend. Add the nopalitos and toss until thoroughly coated. Shake off any excess flour.

In a Dutch oven or deep-fat fryer, heat 2 inches of peanut or corn oil over high heat to 365°F, or until almost smoking. Add the nopalitos to the oil in batches and cook for 1 to 2 minutes, or until golden brown. Using a slotted spoon, transfer to paper towels. Season with salt, arrange in a mound, and serve at once, with salsa, guacamole, or jalapeno jelly alongside. *Makes 4 servings*

*Jars of nopalitos, sliced cactus leaves, or paddles, from the prickly pear cactus, can be found in many grocery stores or at Latino markets.

It is a story, too, of apparent paradoxes and of wonders . . .
It is a place where rain-storms are well nigh unknown, and yet one where
the effects of cloud-bursts are almost unparalleled . . .
It is a region where the beds of lakes are found on the pointed peaks of mountains . . .

—John R. Spears

STUFFED MOJAVE CHICKEN

Spicy chicken breasts stuffed with cheese and chilies. Serve with salsa, wild rice, and a seasonal fresh vegetable.

1 cup shredded queso blanco or mild
    Monterey cheese
2 whole green chilies, chopped
    (one 4-ounce can whole peeled
    green chilies, drained and chopped)
1 1/2 teaspoons ground cumin
1 garlic clove, minced
Tabasco sauce, salt, and freshly ground
    pepper to taste
4 boneless chicken breast halves

SPICE RUB
Juice of 1/2 lime
1 tablespoon pure chile powder
2 garlic cloves, minced
Pinch of sugar
1 teaspoon salt

2 tablespoons olive oil

🌿 Preheat the oven to 400°F. In a medium bowl, combine the cheese, chilies, cumin, garlic, Tabasco, salt, and pepper. Refrigerate for 30 minutes.

🌿 Cut a horizontal slice in each chicken breast and use your fingers to spread open the pockets. Stuff each pocket with the cheese mixture.

🌿 To make the rub: In a small bowl, combine all the ingredients. Stir to make a paste. Rub the chicken breasts with the paste to coat evenly.

🌿 In a large, ovenproof frying pan over medium-high heat, heat the olive oil until almost smoking. Add the chicken breasts, skin side down, and cook for 2 minutes. Turn the chicken over, transfer the pan to the preheated oven, and bake for 15 minutes, or until the chicken is opaque throughout. *Makes 4 servings*

CHOCOLATE TRUFFLES

Luxurious, easy-to-make truffles can be made with various flavorings and sprinkled with complementary toppings. For instance, top amaretto-flavored truffles with chopped almonds, Kahlúa-flavored truffles with chopped white chocolate, and Cognac-flavored truffles with cocoa powder.

12 ounces semisweet chocolate,
   chopped
$^1/_2$ cup heavy cream
2 tablespoons amaretto, Kahlúa, or
   Cognac
3 tablespoons unsalted butter, melted

1 cup unsweetened cocoa powder
4 ounces unsweetened chocolate,
   chopped
Chopped almonds, chopped white
   chocolate, or unsweetened cocoa
   powder for garnish (optional)

🍀 In a double boiler, melt the semisweet chocolate over barely simmering water.

🍀 In a small saucepan, bring the cream to a boil over medium heat; remove from heat and stir in the liqueur or Cognac.

🍀 In a medium bowl, combine the melted butter, melted chocolate, and hot cream mixture. Stir to blend. Let cool. Cover and refrigerate until thickened enough to roll into balls.

🍀 Line a baking sheet with parchment paper or aluminum foil. Using a teaspoon or melon baller, scoop out the chocolate mixture. Roll the chocolate scoops into balls and dredge them in the cocoa powder to coat evenly.

🍀 In a double boiler over barely simmering water, melt the unsweetened chocolate. Quickly dip the truffles in the melted chocolate and set on the prepared baking sheet. If desired, sprinkle the truffles with the almonds, white chocolate, or cocoa. *Makes about 32 truffles*

MAYNARD DIXON *Eagle's Roost* 1927–1946 National Museum of Wildlife Art

THE LODGE AT KOELE

LANAI, HAWAII

From misty mountaintop forests where axis deer roam freely to untouched white sand beaches with exceptionally clear coastal waters, Lanai's natural beauty sets the stage for an unsurpassed experience. The Lodge at Koele is a luxurious upcountry resort that is the ideal starting point for exploring Hawaii's most secluded island. The art-filled lodge combines the refined atmosphere of a plantation owner's home with the warmth and traditional comfort of old Hawaii. The Lodge at Koele has been named by *Condé Nast Traveler* magazine as one of the Best Places to Stay in the World.

Lanai is a small island with two dramatically different environments. Only nine miles separate the tranquil forests that cover the island's upland interior from the miles of tropical beaches and steep sea cliffs of its coastline. There are more than 89,000 acres of wilderness, and Manele Bay and Hulupo'e Bay are part of a Marine Life Conservation District, which is a preferred habitat for Hawaiian spinner dolphins.

With the advent of the pineapple industry and the importation of plantation workers to Lanai in the early 1900s, the island's population changed from pure Hawaiian to an ethnic mixture that includes people of Filipino, Korean, Japanese, Chinese, Anglo-European and Portuguese descent. Lanai City was built in 1924 by the Hawaiian Pineapple Company, later known as Dole Pineapple, and has been left largely intact, a rustic vision of Lanai history. Today, 98 percent of the island is privately owned, and development and tourism are being carefully managed. In 1986, David H. Murdock conceived the idea for the Lodge at Koele, and the lodge was completed in 1990. The island has only two luxury resorts, the upcountry Lodge at Koele and the beachfront Manele Bay Hotel.

Koele was the historic center for ranching operations on the island, and today's lodge guests can saddle up at the stables for a ride through guava forests and ironwood groves or

MENU

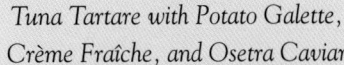

Tuna Tartare with Potato Galette, Crème Fraîche, and Osetra Caviar

Roasted Rack of Lamb with Hazelnut Spoon Bread, Cherry Sauce, and Braised Red Chard

Coconut Cake with Pineapple Ice Cream and Pistachio Meringue

through the plantation hayfields. Hiking, mountain biking, sporting clays, tennis, lawn bowling, croquet, and historical tours are all possible. Two world-famous golf courses, including the championship Experience at Ko'ele, make Lanai a golfer's paradise. Guests can also enjoy the Manele Bay Hotel, where the coral reef attracts colorful tropical fish in a bay prized by divers and snorkelers as one of the best in the world. Popular activities include deep-sea fishing, scuba diving, whale watching in season, rejuvenating spa treatments, and lounging by the pool.

Back at the Lodge at Koele, wicker lounge chairs cushioned with traditional Hawaiian quilted pillows are a marvelous place to sit and watch mist fall over the highlands from spacious verandas. Guests enjoy strolling on pathways that meander among serene flowering gardens with decorative sculptures, lovely fountains, and a large reflecting pond. Orchids are cultivated in the English conservatory, and there is an eighteen-hole putting

course set in a grove of sprawling banyans. At the Lodge's ongoing Visiting Artist Program, guests meet and mingle with celebrated chefs, authors, and musicians.

The Great Hall is the focal point of the grand lodge, and massive stone fireplaces anchor each end of the stately English-country-house-style room. Lanai artists have painted murals, ceiling borders, and floor decorations that portray the flowers, birds, and wildlife of the island, and the room is filled with over-sized furniture and an eclectic collection of paintings, sculptures, and artifacts from around the world. Guests stop here for conversation and a place to relax before or after enjoying a superb meal. Just off the Great Hall, the casual Terrace Restaurant has views of formal English-style gardens and offers American cuisine with Hawaiian influences at breakfast, lunch, and dinner.

In the romantic formal Dining Room, guests are warmed by a crackling fire and dine by candlelight. Executive chef Bradley Czajka's award-winning seasonal menus feature contemporary American cuisine and use the best produce, seafood, and game that Hawaii has to offer. His refined, creative cooking showcases the fresh flavors of the Pacific. After dinner, Hawaiian music is performed by local musicians in the Great Hall. Chef Bradley Czajka created the following recipes and presented them to Menus and Music.

Guests come to the Lodge at Koele for a change in the rhythm of their lives, and after a stay at this grand country retreat surrounded by luxuriant natural beauty, they return home rested and rejuvenated.

This Lodge will be a special place,

a very personal statement of gracious living, elegant dining, and

a home for fine art, and this fine art will be Lana'i art.

—David H. Murdock

TUNA TARTARE WITH POTATO GALETTE, CRÈME FRAÎCHE, AND OSETRA CAVIAR

At the Lodge at Koele, chef Bradley Czajka uses a layer of ahi tuna and a layer of hamachi tuna in this elegant first course. If hamachi is unavailable, use ahi for both layers.

ORANGE-CHIVE VINAIGRETTE
2 tablespoons minced shallot
1 teaspoon minced garlic
Grated zest and juice of 1/2 orange
1/4 cup Champagne vinegar
3/4 cup extra-virgin olive oil
2 tablespoons chopped fresh chives

3 ounces ahi tuna, minced
3 ounces hamachi tuna, minced
Salt and freshly ground pepper to taste
4 potato galettes (see Basics)
4 tablespoons crème fraîche
    (see Basics)
4 teaspoons osetra caviar
8 chives for garnish
Chive Oil (recipe follows)

To make the orange-chive vinaigrette: In a medium bowl, whisk together all the ingredients except the chives. Fold in the chives.

In a small bowl, separately toss each kind of tuna with enough orange-chive vinaigrette to lightly coat. Season with salt and pepper. Place a ring mold on a serving plate and spread one-fourth of the ahi tuna evenly in the bottom. Top with a potato galette. Spread the galette with one-fourth of the hamachi tuna, then 1 tablespoon crème fraîche. Dollop with a 1 teaspoon of caviar and remove the ring mold. Repeat to make 4 molds. Garnish each plate with drizzles of chive oil. Garnish each mold with 2 chives and serve at once. *Makes 4 servings*

CHIVE OIL

1 bunch fresh chives
1/2 cup grapeseed oil or light olive oil

Salt and freshly ground pepper to taste

Cook the chives in a small saucepan of boiling water for 30 seconds. Remove and immediately transfer to a bowl of ice water or rinse under cold water. Squeeze the chives dry and coarsely chop. In a blender, combine the chives, oil, salt, and pepper and purée. *Makes about 3/4 cup*

ROASTED RACK OF LAMB WITH HAZELNUT SPOON BREAD, CHERRY SAUCE, AND BRAISED RED CHARD

Tender, flavorful lamb served on a bed of comforting spoon bread. The luscious sauce and braised chard provide delicious counterpoint.

2 tablespoons olive oil, plus more for chard

Four 4-bone racks of lamb, or two 8-bone racks

2 bunches red chard, stemmed and chopped

Hazelnut Spoon Bread (recipe follows)

Cherry Sauce (recipe follows)

4 sprigs fresh rosemary for garnish

✿ Preheat the oven to 400°F. In a large frying pan, heat the 2 tablespoons olive oil until almost smoking and brown the lamb on both sides. Transfer the pan to the preheated oven and roast for 25 minutes, or until an instant-read thermometer registers 145°F for medium-rare. Remove from the oven and cover loosely with aluminum foil. Slice each rack into 4 chops.

✿ Meanwhile, film a large frying pan with olive oil, heat over medium-high heat, and sauté the chard for 10 minutes, or until tender. Set aside and keep warm.

✿ Place a large spoonful of the spoon bread just above the center of each of 4 plates. Arrange the chard to the side of the spoon bread. Arrange the 4 chops in front and drizzle each plate with the dried cherry sauce. Garnish with a rosemary sprig and serve at once. *Makes 4 servings*

HAZELNUT SPOON BREAD

2 ears of corn, husked

2 cups milk

1/2 cup (1 stick) unsalted butter, cut into pieces

1/4 cup sugar

3 tablespoons cornmeal

2 tablespoons masa harina

1 tablespoon flour

1 tablespoon baking powder

1 teaspoon salt

2 eggs

2 cups half-and-half

1 cup hazelnuts, toasted, skinned, and ground (see Basics)

(continued)

🌿 Using the large rasps of a box grater, grate each ear of corn into a shallow bowl. You should have 1 cup corn purée.

🌿 In a large saucepan, combine the milk, butter, and sugar. Bring to a boil over medium heat and cook until the butter melts. Whisk in the cornmeal, masa harina, flour, and corn purée and cook, whisking constantly, until the mixture returns to a boil. Continue cooking for 2 minutes, then remove from heat and let cool.

🌿 Preheat the oven to 350°F. Butter an 8-inch square baking dish.

🌿 In a large bowl, whisk the cooled corn mixture, baking powder, salt, and eggs together until blended. Whisk in the half-and-half until blended. Fold in the ground nuts. Pour into the prepared baking dish and bake in the preheated oven for 45 minutes, or until a skewer inserted in the center comes out almost clean. *Makes 4 servings*

CHERRY SAUCE

1/2 cup plus 3 tablespoons dried sweet cherries
1 tablespoon olive oil
3 tablespoons diced shallots
1 small carrot, peeled and diced
1 small celery stalk, diced
1/2 leek, white part only, diced

1/2 parsnip, peeled and diced
1/2 cup dry red wine
1/2 cup lamb or veal demi-glace*
2 cups chicken stock (see Basics) or canned low-salt chicken broth
2 fresh thyme sprigs
1 tablespoon unsalted butter

🌿 Put the 1/2 cup cherries in a medium bowl, add hot water to cover, and let stand for 20 to 30 minutes, or until plump. Drain and finely chop.

🌿 In a medium saucepan over medium-high heat, heat the olive oil and sauté the 3 tablespoons cherries, the shallots, carrot, celery, leek, and parsnip until they begin to brown. Stir in the red wine. Add the demi-glace, stock or broth, and thyme and simmer for 20 to 25 minutes, or until the liquid is reduced by one-third. Season with salt and pepper and strain through a fine-mesh sieve. Bring the sauce to a boil and stir in the chopped cherries. Remove from heat and whisk in the butter. *Makes about 2 1/2 cups*

*Frozen lamb or veal demi-glace is available at some grocery stores and specialty foods markets.

THE LODGE AT KOELE

COCONUT CAKE WITH PINEAPPLE ICE CREAM AND PISTACHIO MERINGUE

Fabulous tropical flavors and a stylish presentation combine in this light, elegant dessert. The ice cream can also be made with guava or mango purée.

Pineapple Ice Cream (recipe follows)

COCONUT CAKE

4 eggs, separated

9 tablespoons granulated sugar

$^1/_2$ teaspoon vanilla extract

$1^1/_4$ cups all-purpose flour

$^1/_2$ cup packed sweetened shredded dried coconut

PISTACHIO MERINGUES

2 egg whites

4 tablespoons granulated sugar

$^1/_4$ cup powdered sugar

$^1/_4$ cup finely ground pistachios

12 thin slices fresh pineapple

12 tablespoons sugar for sprinkling

Fresh edible flowers and chopped pistachios for garnish

To make the coconut cake: Preheat the oven to 375°F. Line the bottom of an 8-inch square cake pan with parchment paper and set aside.

In a large bowl, combine the egg whites, 2 tablespoons of the sugar, and $^1/_4$ teaspoon of the vanilla extract. Beat until soft peaks form. Gradually add 5 tablespoons of the sugar, beating until stiff, glossy peaks form.

In a medium bowl, combine the egg yolks, the remaining 2 tablespoons sugar, and the remaining $^1/_4$ teaspoon vanilla extract; beat until pale.

Fold the egg yolk mixture into the egg whites. Gradually fold in the flour and coconut. Spread the batter in the prepared cake pan and bake in the preheated oven for 12 to 15 minutes, or until a skewer inserted in the center comes out clean. Remove from the oven and let cool on a wire rack.

To make the pistachio meringues: Preheat the oven to 225°F. Butter a baking sheet or line it with parchment paper.

(continued)

In a medium bowl, beat the egg whites and 2 tablespoons of the granulated sugar until soft peaks form. Add the remaining 2 tablespoons granulated sugar and beat until stiff, glossy peaks form. Fold in the powdered sugar and ground pistachios. Using a pastry bag fitted with a large plain tip, pipe 2-inch squares of meringue onto the baking sheet, or drop by tablespoonfuls and use a knife to square up the sides. Bake in the preheated oven for about 1 hour, or until the meringues are firm and dry on the outside but have not colored.

Evenly spread the ice cream over the top of the coconut cake. Freeze the cake for at least 2 hours or overnight. Cut into 2-inch square pieces.

To serve, preheat the broiler. Place the pineapple slices on a baking sheet, sprinkle evenly with sugar, and broil 2 inches from the heat source until caramelized. Place a thin slice of pineapple on each plate. Arrange a square of cake on top of each pineapple slice. Top the ice cream with a pistachio meringue. Garnish with fresh flowers, sprinkle the plate with a few chopped pistachios, and serve at once. *Makes 16 servings*

PINEAPPLE ICE CREAM

2 cups heavy cream
$1^1/2$ cups granulated sugar
5 egg yolks

$1/4$ vanilla bean, split lengthwise,
    or $1/2$ teaspoon vanilla extract
$1^1/2$ cups pineapple purée

In a large saucepan, combine the cream and sugar. Stir over medium heat until almost boiling; remove from heat. In a medium bowl, whisk the egg yolks until pale. Gradually whisk in half of the hot cream mixture. Add the vanilla bean, if using. Return to the saucepan and cook over medium heat, stirring constantly, until thickened, about 5 minutes. Do not boil. Remove from heat. Let cool. Remove the vanilla pod, if used, or stir in the vanilla extract, if using. Cover and refrigerate until chilled, at least 2 hours. Stir the pineapple purée into the chilled custard. Freeze in an ice cream maker according to the manufacturer's instructions. *Makes 1 quart*

MICHAEL CARROL *The Lodge at Koele* 2002

BASICS

ANCHO CHILI PURÉE

2 ancho chilies

In a small bowl, soak the ancho chilies in hot water for 20 minutes. In a food processor, purée the chilies with 2 teaspoons water until smooth.

BOURBON CUSTARD SAUCE

2 cups milk
$^{1}/_{2}$ vanilla bean, split lengthwise, or
  1 teaspoon vanilla extract

4 egg yolks
$^{3}/_{4}$ cup sugar
2 tablespoons bourbon

Add the milk to a medium, heavy saucepan and scrape the seeds from the vanilla bean into the milk; add the pod. Bring just to a simmer over low heat. Remove from heat and let stand for 20 minutes to infuse the milk with vanilla flavor. Scrape the vanilla bean pod again and add the scrapings to the milk; discard the pod.

In a medium bowl, whisk the egg yolks and sugar together until pale. Gradually whisk in the hot milk. Return to the pan and cook over low heat, stirring constantly, until the custard thickens enough to coat the back of a spoon. Strain through a fine-mesh sieve into a medium bowl and stir in the vanilla extract, if using, and the bourbon. Let cool, then refrigerate the custard until chilled. *Makes about 2 cups*

CLARIFIED BUTTER

Clarified butter is used for cooking at high temperatures, as it will not burn. In a small, heavy saucepan, melt unsalted butter over low heat. Remove the pan from heat and let stand for several minutes. Skim off the foam and pour off the clear liquid, leaving the milky solids in the bottom of the pan. Cover and store in the refrigerator indefinitely. When clarified, butter loses about one-fourth of its original volume.

CRÈME FRAÎCHE

2 cups heavy cream   2 tablespoons buttermilk

In a medium bowl, whisk the ingredients together. Cover with plastic wrap and let sit covered at room temperature overnight or until fairly thick. Refrigerate for at least 4 hours. The cream can be kept in the refrigerator for several days. *Makes 2 cups*

CROSTINI

Cut 1 day-old French baguette into $1/4$-inch-thick slices. Brush each slice lightly with olive oil on one side. Arrange the bread on a baking sheet and bake in a preheated 375°F oven for about 10 minutes, or until lightly golden; let cool. Store in an airtight container. *Makes 36 toasts*

FRUIT SALSA

1 cup chopped mixed fresh fruits, such as grapes, kiwi, mango, papaya, pineapple, peach, and/or raspberries
1 small handful fresh cilantro leaves, chopped

1 tablespoon balsamic vinegar
1 tablespoon brown sugar
Cayenne pepper to taste

In a medium bowl, combine all the ingredients. Set aside to let the flavors blend. *Makes 1 cup*

GUACAMOLE

1 large ripe avocado, halved and pitted
Juice of 1 lime
$1/2$ tomato, seeded and chopped
1 small handful fresh cilantro leaves, chopped

$1/4$ red onion, finely chopped
1 jalapeno chili, seeded and finely chopped (optional)
Salt to taste

In a medium bowl, combine all the ingredients and gently mash with a fork. Serve at room temperature. *Makes $1^1/2$ cups*

LIME SOUR CREAM

$^1/_2$ cup sour cream

1 tablespoon fresh lime juice

Salt to taste

In a small bowl, combine all the ingredients. Cover and refrigerate until ready to use. *Makes $^1/_2$ cup*

PESTO

1 cup chopped fresh basil

1 garlic clove

$^1/_3$ cup extra-virgin olive oil

1 tablespoon pine nuts

2 tablespoons grated Parmesan cheese

In a blender or food processor, purée all of the ingredients until smooth. Use immediately, or cover with olive oil and refrigerate for up to 3 days. *Makes about $^1/_2$ cup*

POTATO GALETTES

2 baking potatoes,

$^1/_4$ cup clarified butter (see Basics) or olive oil

1 teaspoon salt

$^1/_2$ teaspoon freshly ground pepper

Scrub the potatoes and steam for 12 to 15 minutes, or until just barely cooked through. Let cool, uncovered, and refrigerate until cold. Peel and grate the potatoes onto a baking sheet; toss with salt and pepper.

In a large frying pan over medium-high heat, heat 2 tablespoons of the butter or olive oil. Drop $^1/_2$ cup of the potato mixture into the pan to make 3 galettes. Sauté for 4 to 5 minutes, pressing the potatoes together with a spatula, until the bottom has crusted and browned. Flip over, and sauté to brown the other side a few minutes more. Keep warm while finishing the rest. *Makes about 6 galettes*

ROASTED GARLIC

Preheat the oven to 375°F. Using a sharp knife, slice the top off a garlic bulb to expose the tops of the cloves. Drizzle the exposed cloves with 1 tablespoon olive oil. Tightly wrap the bulb in aluminum foil and bake in the preheated oven for 45 minutes, or until soft. Let cool, then squeeze the cloves to remove the pulp.

ROASTING PEPPERS AND CHILIES

Roast whole peppers or chilies on a grill, directly over the flame on a gas stove, or in a cast-iron frying pan over medium-high heat, turning to char on all sides. Or, cut large peppers or chilies into fourths, seed, press to flatten, and char under a preheated broiler very close to the heat source. Using tongs, transfer the peppers or chilies to a paper bag, close it, and let the peppers or chilies cool for 10 to 15 minutes. Remove from the bag, peel off the skin with your fingers or a small, sharp knife, and core and seed the peppers or chilies if charred whole.

SALSA

4 tomatoes, diced
1 jalapeno chili, seeded and minced
1 habanero chili, seeded and minced
  (optional)

$1/2$ red onion, finely chopped
$1/4$ cup minced fresh cilantro
Salt and freshly ground pepper to taste
Juice of $1/2$ lime, or more to taste

In a medium bowl, combine the tomato, jalapeno, optional habanero, red onion, and cilantro. Let sit for 15 minutes. Drain off any excess liquid. Stir in the salt, pepper, and lime juice. *Makes about 2 cups*

SHREDDING FRESH BASIL

Stack fresh basil leaves and roll them up like a jelly roll. Cut into thin crosswise slices.

TOASTING NUTS

Spread the nuts on a baking sheet and bake in a preheated 350°F oven, stirring once or twice, for 5 to 10 minutes, or until fragrant and very lightly browned.

TOASTING AND SKINNING HAZELNUTS

Preheat the oven to 350°F. Spread the hazelnuts on a baking sheet and bake in the preheated oven for 10 minutes, or until fragrant and very lightly browned. Transfer to a clean towel and rub to remove most of the skins.

VANILLA SAUCE

1/2 cup milk

1/2 cup heavy cream

1/2 vanilla bean, split lengthwise, or
   1 teaspoon vanilla extract

2 tablespoons sugar

2 egg yolks

In a medium saucepan, bring the milk, cream, and vanilla bean, if using, to a boil over medium-high heat. Remove from heat and stir in the sugar. In a medium bowl, whisk the sugar and egg yolks together until pale. Gradually pour one-third of the milk mixture into the egg mixture, whisking constantly. Return to the saucepan. Cook over medium heat, stirring constantly, until the mixture thickens enough to coat the back of the spoon. Remove from heat. Remove the vanilla bean, or stir in the vanilla extract, if using. Transfer the sauce to a bowl, let cool, and refrigerate until chilled. *Makes about 1 cup*

WARMING PLATES

Preheat the oven to 200°F. Warm plates in the preheated oven for 10 minutes.

STOCKS

BEEF STOCK

4 pounds meaty beef bones, sliced

2 tablespoons olive oil

1 onion, chopped

1 bay leaf

3 fresh flat-leaf parsley sprigs

6 black peppercorns

1/2 cup dry white wine

3 quarts water

1/2 cup tomato purée

Salt and freshly ground pepper to taste

Preheat the oven to 400°F. In a roasting pan, toss the bones with the olive oil to coat evenly. Roast for 40 minutes, or until well browned, turning occasionally. Transfer to a stockpot.

Pour the fat out of the roasting pan. Place the pan over medium heat, add the wine, and stir to scrape up the browned bits from the bottom of the pan. Pour this liquid into the stockpot. Add all the remaining ingredients. Bring to a boil and skim off any foam that rises to the top. Simmer slowly, uncovered, for 3 to 4 hours, or until the stock is well flavored.

Strain through a fine-mesh sieve into a bowl and let cool. Cover and refrigerate overnight. Remove and discard the congealed fat on the surface. Store in the refrigerator for up to 3 days. To keep longer, bring to a boil every 3 days or freeze for up to 3 months. *Makes about 4 cups*

CHICKEN STOCK

2 onions, coarsely chopped
Bouquet garni: 4 parsley sprigs,
  4 peppercorns, 1 thyme sprig, and
  1 bay leaf, tied in a cheesecloth
  square

4 pounds chicken bones and bony
  parts such as backs, necks, and wings
2 carrots, peeled and chopped
3 celery stocks, chopped
5 garlic cloves

In a stockpot, combine all the ingredients and add water to cover by 2 inches. Bring to a boil and skim off any foam that forms on the surface. Reduce heat to low and simmer, uncovered, for $1^1/2$ to 2 hours, or until the stock is well flavored. Strain through a fine-mesh sieve and let cool completely. Cover and refrigerate overnight. Remove and discard any congealed fat on the surface. Store in the refrigerator for up to 3 days. To keep longer, bring to a boil every 3 days, or freeze for up to 3 months. *Makes about 6 cups*

DUCK STOCK

3 pounds duck bones and trimmings,
  rinsed
1 cup dry wine
1 onion, chopped
1 large carrot, peeled and chopped

1 celery stock, chopped
1 leek, including some of the green
  leaves, chopped
9 fresh parsley sprigs
Salt and freshly ground pepper to taste

Preheat the oven to 450°F. Add the bones and trimmings to a roasting pan and bake in the preheated oven, turning once or twice, for 30 minutes, or until deep brown. Transfer to a stockpot and drain the fat from the roasting pan.

Place the roasting pan over medium heat and add the wine to the pan. Stir to scrape up the browned bits. Add this liquid to the stockpot along with the onion, carrot, celery, leek, and parsley. Add water to cover by 1 inch and bring to a boil over high heat. Skim the surface to remove any foam that rises to the top. Reduce heat to a simmer and cook uncovered for 3 to 4 hours, adding water as needed to keep the ingredients covered. Add salt and pepper. Strain through a fine-mesh sieve. Cover and refrigerate for several hours. Remove and discard any congealed fat. Store in the refrigerator for up to 3 days. To keep longer, bring to a boil every 3 days, or freeze for up to 3 months. *Makes about 6 cups*

FISH STOCK

4 pounds heads and bones of white-
    fleshed fish such as sole or whiting,
    cut up
8 cups water
1 carrot, peeled and sliced
2 onions, chopped
1 celery stalk, sliced
Bouquet garni: 6 parsley stems,
    4 peppercorns, 1 fresh thyme sprig,
    and 1 bay leaf, tied in a cheesecloth
    square
1 cup dry white wine

In a stockpot, combine the fish heads, bones, and water. Bring to a boil, skimming off the scum that rises to the surface. Reduce heat to low, add all the remaining ingredients, and simmer, uncovered, for 30 minutes. Remove from heat and strain through a sieve into a large saucepan. Bring to a boil and cook to reduce the liquid by about one third. Use now, or let cool completely, cover, and refrigerate for up to 2 days. To keep longer, bring to a boil every 2 days, or freeze for up to 2 months. *Makes about 8 cups*

VEGETABLE STOCK

1 cup coarsely chopped carrot
1 cup chopped celery
2 unpeeled onions, quartered, or 2
    leeks, cleaned and chopped
1 cup peeled and chopped parsnip
1 cup peeled and chopped rutabaga or
    turnip
2 cups vegetable scraps and trimmings
2 or 3 fresh parsley sprigs
1 or 2 bay leaves
$1/2$ teaspoon minced fresh thyme
$1/2$ teaspoon ground pepper
8 cups water, or more as needed

In a large stockpot, combine all the ingredients and bring to a boil. Reduce heat to low and simmer for 1 to 2 hours. Remove from heat and strain through a fine-mesh sieve.

    Cover and refrigerate for up to 3 days. To keep longer, bring the stock to a boil every 3 days, or freeze for up to 3 months. *Makes about 8 cups*

CONVERSION CHART

WEIGHT MEASUREMENTS

STANDARD U.S.	OUNCES	METRIC
1 ounce	1	30 g
$1/4$ pound	4	125 g
$1/2$ pound	8	250 g
1 pound	16	500 g
$1^1/2$ pounds	24	750 g
2 pounds	32	1 kg
$2^1/2$ pounds	40	1.25 kg
3 pounds	48	1.5 kg

VOLUME MEASUREMENTS

STANDARD U.S.	FLUID OUNCES	METRIC
1 tablespoon	$1/2$	15 ml
2 tablespoons	1	30 ml
3 tablespoons	$1^1/2$	45 ml
$1/4$ cup (4 tablespoons)	2	60 ml
6 tablespoons	3	90 ml
$1/2$ cup (8 tablespoons)	4	125 ml
1 cup	8	250 ml
1 pint (2 cups)	16	500 ml
4 cups	32	1 l

OVEN TEMPERATURES

FAHRENHEIT	CELSIUS	GAS MARK
250°	120°	$1/2$
275°	135°	1
300°	150°	2
325°	165°	3
350°	180°	4
375°	190°	5
400°	200°	6
425°	220°	7

Note: For ease of use, measurements have been rounded off.

CONVERSION FACTORS

OUNCES TO GRAMS: Multiply the ounce figure by 28.3 to get the number of grams.

POUNDS TO GRAMS: Multiply the pound figure by 453.59 to get the number of grams.

POUNDS TO KILOGRAMS: Multiply the pound figure by 0.45 to get the number of kilograms.

OUNCES TO MILLILITERS: Multiply the ounce figure by 30 to get the number of milliliters.

CUPS TO LITERS: Multiply the cup figure by 0.24 to get the number of liters.

FAHRENHEIT TO CELSIUS: Subtract 32 from the Fahrenheit figure, multiply by 5, then divide by 9 to get the Celsius figure.

CONTRIBUTORS AND NATIONAL PARKS

BAR HARBOR INN
Newport Drive
Bar Harbor, ME 04609
(800) 248-3351 or (207) 288-3351
www.barharborinn.com

LAKE PLACID LODGE
Whiteface Inn Road
P.O. Box 550
Lake Placid, NY 12946
(877) 523-2700 or (518) 523-2700
www.lakeplacidlodge.com

**GLENDORN, A LODGE IN
THE COUNTRY**
1032 West Corydon Street
Bradford, PA 16701
(800) 843-8568 or (814) 362-6511
www.glendorn.com

THE SWAG
2300 Swag Road
Waynesville, NC 28785
(800) 789-7672 or (828) 926-0430
www.theswag.com

CANOE BAY
P.O. Box 28
Chetek, WI 54728
(800) 568-1995 or (715) 924-4594
www.canoebay.com

CIBOLO CREEK RANCH
P.O. Box 44
Shafter, TX 79850
(866) 496-9460 or (915) 229-3737
www.cibolocreekranch.com

THE HOME RANCH
P.O. Box 822
Clark, CO 80428
(970) 879-1780
www.homeranch.com

THE LODGE AT VAIL
174 East Gore Creek Drive
Vail, CO 81657
(800) 331-5634 or (970) 476-5011
www.lodgeatvail.rockresorts.com

THE LAKE YELLOWSTONE HOTEL
P.O. Box 165
Yellowstone National Park, WY 82190
(307) 344-7311
www.travelyellowstone.com

JENNY LAKE LODGE
P.O. Box 250
Moran, WY 83013
(800) 628-9988 or (307) 543-3100
www.gtlc.com/lodgeJen.htm

JACKSON LAKE LODGE
P.O. Box 250
Moran, WY 83013
(800) 628-9988 or (307) 543-3100
www.gtlc.com/lodgeJac.htm

SUNDANCE
Rural Route No. 3 Box A-1
Sundance, UT 84604
(800) 892-1600 or (801) 225-4107
www.sundanceresort.com

BRYCE CANYON LODGE
Bryce Canyon National Park
UT, 84717
(888) 297-2757 or (303) 297-2757
www.brycecanyonlodge.com

ZION LODGE
Zion National Park
Springdale, UT 84767
(888) 297-2757 or (303) 297-2757
www.zionlodge.com

GRAND CANYON LODGE
Grand Canyon National Park
North Rim, AZ 86052
(888) 297-2757 or (303) 297-2757
www.grandcanyonnorthrim.com

EL TOVAR
P.O. Box 699
Grand Canyon, AZ 86023
(888) 297-2757 or (303) 297-2757
www.grandcanyonlodges.com

TIMBERLINE LODGE
Timberline Lodge, OR 97028
(800) 547-1406 or (503) 622-7979
www.timberlinelodge.com

THE AHWAHNEE HOTEL
One Ahwahnee Road
Yosemite National Park, CA 95389
(209) 372-1407
www.yosemitepark.com

FURNACE CREEK INN
P.O. Box 1
Highway 190
Death Valley, CA 92328
(760) 786-2345 or (303) 297-2757
www.furnacecreekresort.com

LODGE AT KOELE
P.O. Box 630310
Lanai City, HI 96763
(800) 321-4666 or (808) 565-7300
www.lodgeatkoele.com

ACADIA NATIONAL PARK
(207) 288-3338
www.nps.gov/acad

**GREAT SMOKY MOUNTAINS
NATIONAL PARK**
(865) 436-1200
www.nps.gov/grsm

BIG BEND NATIONAL PARK
(915) 477-2251
www.nps.gov/bibe

YELLOWSTONE NATIONAL PARK
(307) 344-7381
www.nps.gov/yell

GRAND TETON NATIONAL PARK
(307) 739-3300
www.nps.gov/grte

BRYCE CANYON NATIONAL PARK
(435) 834-5322
www.nps.gov/brca

ZION NATIONAL PARK
(435) 772-3256
www.nps.gov/zion

GRAND CANYON NATIONAL PARK
(928) 638-7888
www.nps.gov/grca

YOSEMITE NATIONAL PARK
(209) 372-0200
www.nps.gov/yose

DEATH VALLEY NATIONAL PARK
(760) 786-3200
www.nps.gov/deva

**NATIONAL PARK SERVICE
HEADQUARTERS**
(888) 467-2757
www.nps.gov

ACKNOWLEDGMENTS

I would like to thank the many people who made this volume possible. My deepest gratitude to the lodge owners, managers, and chefs who generously contributed recipes to the cookbook: David J. Witham, Louis Kiefer, Jill Reeves; David and Christie Garrett, Sean Mohammed, Kathryn Kincannon; Dan and Audrey Abrashoff, Diarmuid Murphy; Dan and Deener Matthews, Matthew Frey, Mindy Wood; Lisa and Dan Dobrowolski, Scott Johnson; Pat Gleason, Johnny D, Griselda Machaca; Ken Jones, Clyde Nelson; Wolfgang Triebnig, Thomas J. Newsted; Bo Cleveland; Angela Beaumont, Wes Hamilton; Joseph A. Santangini; Robert Redford, Jason Knibb, Keith Archibald, Larry Callahan, Kendall Wimer; Les Garvin, Joyce Caps; Jim Fendrick, Mark Kleyla; Bruce Brossman, Joe Nobile, Don Botta, Jeff D'Arpa; Richard and Jeff Kohnstamm, Leif Benson, Jon Tullis, Linny Adamson, Randy Black; Kevin Kelly for giving me the idea in the first place, Jim Anile, Doug Dirksen, Andrea Fulton; Cal and Toni Jepson, Michelle Hanson; David H. Murdock, Tina Harlow, Bradley Czajka.

Affectionate thanks to musicians Jim Nichols, Bobby Black, Rich Kuhns, Chris Kranyak, Michael Bluestein, Paul van Wageningen, and Peter Barshay. I am forever grateful to Peter Barshay and Jim Nichols for their arrangements and to Peter for rounding up the tunes. Thanks also to engineer Dave Luke, George Horn, and Nina Bombardier of Fantasy Studios, Berkeley.

Once again, sincere thanks to Paul Moore for his stunning food photography, Amy Nathan for her extraordinary food styling, and Sara Slavin for her stylish tableware.

Very special thanks to Tom and Mona Mesereau, of Mesereau Public Relations. Thanks to Debra Kaiser, Claudia Wade, Marsha Karle, Annette Hartigan, Mary Kay Manning, Kieth Waldon, Tim Tan, Kristi Leavitt, Jim Williams, Carrie Thorpe, Lisa Bishop, Jan Stock, Lucy Ridolphi, Dennis Reason, Mike Buchetti, Maureen Oltrogge, Kerri Holden, Ariel Palmieri, and Sara Moriarty. Thanks to Jim Dodge for his vintage menus and postcards, and to Ann Foster, National Museum of Wildlife Art; Julie Dunn-Morton, Woodcock Museum of the St. Louis Mercantile Library Association; J. Brendan Williams, California Historical Society; Julien Tavener, Haley & Steele galleries; Tracy Meehan, Adirondack Museum; Ranger Doug and Lisa Bergman, Ranger Doug's Enterprises; Lorelie Eurto, Munson Williams Proctor Arts Institute; Barbara Wood, National Gallery of Art; and Sara Hammond, the Frank Lloyd Wright Foundation.

I want to especially acknowledge the work of Sarah Creider and to thank her for sticking with me through thick and thin on this enormous project. Years of heartfelt thank-yous to Sharlene Swacke, Tim Forney, Claire Coreris, Ned Waring, Kirk Crippens, Mary Ann Wetzork, Erick Villatoro, and Isidro Montesinos of Menus and Music.

Deepest gratitude to my longtime editor Carolyn Miller of San Francisco. Thanks to Jennifer Barry and Kristen Wurz of Jennifer Barry Design for the book and cover design.

And, as always, I thank my daughters Claire and Caitlin and my husband John for their love and support.

CREDITS

Front Cover Lake Placid Lodge. **Back Cover** JKM Collection, National Museum of Wildlife Art, Jackson WY, 1987.116. Photography by W. Garth Dowling, Jackson, WY. **p 6** California Historical Society, Gift of William H. Noble. TN-2750. **p 13** California Historical Society. TN-0230. **p 17** (clockwise from upper left) Yellowstone National Park, Works Progress Administration (WPA), c. 1939, Artist Unknown. Artwork and design © Ranger Doug's Enterprises™. Ranger Doug's Enterprises, 2442 NW Market St., #567, Seattle, WA 98107 (888) 972-7678. Library of Congress, Prints & Photographs Division, WPA Poster Collection. LC-USZC2-1015. Zion National Park, Works Progress Administration (WPA), c. 1939, Artist Unknown. Artwork and design © Ranger Doug's Enterprises™. Library of Congress, Prints & Photographs Division, WPA Poster Collection. LC-USZC4-8221. **p 25** Frederic Edwin Church, *Sunset*, 1856. Oil on canvas (24 X 36 in). Munson-Williams-Proctor Arts Institute, Museum of Art, Utica, New York. Quote: © 1956 by Rachel L. Carson, from *The Sense of Wonder* by Rachel Carson (New York: Harper Collins) Reprinted by permission of Frances Collin, trustee. **p 39** August Loeffler *Bolton, Sept. 10th '64*, 1864. Courtesy of the Adirondack Museum. 1994.005.0001. **p 43** Gifford Pinchot, from *Training of a Forester*, revised third edition, 1917. **p 49** Winslow Homer, *Casting, Number Two*, 1894. Gift of Ruth K. Henschel in memory of her husband, Charles R. Henschel. Image © 2003 Board of Trustees, National Gallery of Art, Washington, 1894. **p 50** Photograph by John Warner. **p 52** Great Smoky Mountains National Park. Photograph by Thomas C. Gray, Oct. 1997. **p 53** Great Smoky Mountains National Park. Photograph by E.G. Doldo, May 1993. **p 55** Horace Kephart, *Glimpses of Our National Parks*, 1941 edition (first published in 1915). **p 59** *Great Blue Heron*. After John James Audubon. Etching with aquatint from *Birds of America*, 1827–38. (26¹/4 X 39 in). www.jjaudubon.com. **p 60** Photograph by Michael Grimm. **p 62** (left) Photograph by Layne Kennedy. (right) Photograph by Michael Grimm. **p 63** Frank Lloyd Wright, UC Berkeley, 1957. **p 71** *Yucca and Chisos Mountains*. National Park Service. **p 73** (clockwise from left) *Rafters in Santa Elena Canyon*. National Park Service. *The West Side of the Chisos Mountains*. Photograph by Ro Wauer. *The Rock "Window" at the Chimneys*. National Park Service. Quote: Wallace Stegner, from "The Wilderness Letter," 1960. **p 76** *Great Bittern*. After John James Audubon. Etching with aquatint from *Birds of America*, 1827–38. (26¹/4 X 39 in). www.jjaudubon.com. **p 86** Courtesy of Vail Resorts. Photograph by Dann Coffey. **p 88** Courtesy of Vail Resorts. Photograph by Jack Affleck. Quote: from "The Dreamer" by Mike Anton, published in the *Rocky Mountain News* January 3, 1999. Reprinted with permission of the *Rocky Mountain News*. **p 89** Courtesy of Vail Resorts. Photograph by Jack Affleck. **p 96, 98, 99, 101** Courtesy of National Park Service. **p 105** The Lyle and Aileen Woodcock Museum by arrangement with the Mercantile Library at the University of Missouri–St. Louis. woodcockmuseum.umsl.edu. **p 107** Copyright L. Prang & Co. Library of Congress. LC-USZC4-3246. **p 119** JKM Collection, National Museum of Wildlife Art, Jackson, WY. Photography by W. Garth Dowling, Jackson, WY. **p 123** JKM Collection, National Museum of Wildlife Art, Jackson, WY. Photography by W. Garth Dowling, Jackson, WY. **p 143** The Union Pacific System. *Zion National Park, Grand Canyon National Park, Bryce Canyon National Park, The Cedar Breaks, Kaibab National Forest* (Omaha, Neb.: no publisher given, 1929). **p 159** Bruce Aiken, *Horn Creek Rapids*, 1998. Oil on canvas (40 X 30 in). Collection of Edward Marue, Tucson, AZ. www.bruceaiken.com. **p 171, 172, 177** Courtesy of Friends of Timberline. **p 178, 180, 182, 189** Yosemite Concession Services Corporation. **p 183** Ansel Adams, untitled two-page typewritten document on the Ahwahnee, no date, pp. 1–2. On file at the Yosemite National Park Research Library. **p 186** California Historical Society, TN-4060. **p 194** John R. Spears, *Illustrated Sketches of Death Valley and Other Borax Deserts of the Pacific Coast* (Rand, McNally & Company, 1892). **p 197** Maynard Dixon, *Eagle's Roost*, 1927–46. JKM Collection, National Museum of Wildlife Art, Jackson, WY. Photography by W. Garth Dowling, Jackson, WY. **p 209** Michael Carrol, *The Lodge at Koele*, 2002. Oil on linen (16 X 20 in). www.mikecarrollgallery.com. **p 224** Yosemite Concession Services Corporation

INDEX

A

Acadia National Park 24
Adams, Ansel 183
Ahi Tuna, Macadamia Nut-Crusted, with Crab Risotto and Leek Sauce 91
The Ahwahnee Hotel 179
Appaloosa Bean Chili 187
Appetizers
  Baked Brie 148
  Crisp Cactus 194
  Jalapeno-Hummus Dip 140
  Quesadillas with Brie Cheese, Mango, and Chilies 81
  Smoked Trout Bruschetta 155
  White Bean Purée, Baked Shiitake Mushrooms, and Roasted Red Peppers 100
Apple and Cranberry Cobbler with Vanilla Bean Ice Cream 66
Apple-Butternut Squash Soup 54
Apricot Bavarian Creams with Strawberry-Champagne Soup 114
Arugula, Smoked Salmon, and Toasted Hazelnut Salad 64
Asparagus, Roasted, with Truffle-Mustard Potato Salad 111

B

Bar Harbor Inn 21
Bean Soup with Sausage and Cilantro 44
Beef Tenderloin
  Almond-Crusted, and Garlic Mashed Potatoes 56
  Grilled, with Ranch Tomato Sauce 82
Beets, Roasted, and Three-Bean Salad with Mustard Vinaigrette 130
Big Bend National Park 71
Black Bean
  –Corn Relish 149
  Soup with Lime Sour Cream and Tortilla Strips 163
Blueberry Pie 28
Bourbon Sauce 143
Boysenberry Pie 188
Brie, Baked 148
Bryceberry Bread Pudding with Bourbon Sauce 142
Bryce Canyon Lodge 137
Bryce Canyon National Park 139
Butternut Squash
  –Apple Soup 54
  Purée 133

C

Canoe Bay 61
Carson, Rachel 25
CCC and WPA 16
Cherry Sauce 204

Chicken
  Grilled Southwest, with Black Bean–Corn Relish 148
  Pan-Seared Breast with Chanterelle, Shiitake, and Sherry Sauce 174
  Stuffed Mojave 195
Chili
  Appaloosa Bean 187
  -Lime Rice 165
Chive Oil 202
Chocolate
  Bread Pudding with Bourbon Custard Sauce 85
  Cakes with Chocolate Ice Cream 134
  Coconut Croissant Pudding 48
  Ice Cream 135
  Tart, Orange-Scented, with Chocolate-Tea Sorbet 93
  Truffles 196
Cibolo Creek Ranch 69
Clam Chowder, Astoria 173
Coconut Cake with Pineapple Ice Cream and Pistachio Meringue 206
Corn
  Caramelized 83
  Salsa, Fire-Roasted 165
Crab Risotto 92
Crème Anglaise 48
Crème Brûlée 38
Crisp Cactus Appetizers 194

D

Death Valley National Park 193
Dellenbaugh, Frederick S. 151
Desert
  Blossom 157
  Napoleon with Raspberry Coulis 166
Desserts
  Apple and Cranberry Cobbler with Vanilla Bean Ice Cream 66
  Apricot Bavarian Creams with Strawberry-Champagne Soup 114
  Blueberry Pie 28
  Boysenberry Pie 188
  Bryceberry Bread Pudding with Bourbon Sauce 142
  Coconut Cake with Pineapple Ice Cream and Pistachio Meringue 206
  Chocolate Bread Pudding with Bourbon Custard Sauce 85
  Chocolate and Coconut Croissant Pudding 48
  Chocolate Cakes with Chocolate Ice Cream 134
  Chocolate Tart, Orange-Scented, with Chocolate-Tea Sorbet 93

Chocolate-Tea Sorbet 93
Chocolate Truffles 196
Crème Brûlée 38
Desert Blossom 157
Desert Napoleon with Raspberry Coulis 166
French Crumb Cake with Huckleberry Sauce 106
Granola Crème Brûlée 150
Huckleberry Ice Cream 58
Marionberry-Ginger Crisp with Kirsch-Hazelnut Streusel 176
Mocha Flans with Caramel Sauce and English Toffee 124
Tres Leches Cake 77
Dessert Sauces
  Bourbon Custard Sauce 210
  Bourbon Sauce 143
  Crème Anglaise 48
  Huckleberry Sauce 107
  Raspberry Coulis 167
Duck
  Breast, Roast, with Black Pepper Curry 36
  Breast Roulade, with Cognac Sauce, Polenta, and Haricots Verts 102
  Prosciutto with Caramelized Pears and Balsamic Glaze 120

E

El Tovar 161

F

Fish
  Ahi Tuna, Macadamia Nut–Crusted, with Crab Risotto and Leek Sauce 91
  Halibut Fillets, Pan-Seared, on Shrimp and Lobster Potato Cakes with Corn Salsa and Chili Butter Sauce 46
  Red Trout Fillets, Pan-Fried 140
  Salmon, Tostadas with Fire-Roasted Corn Salsa 164
  Tuna Tartare with Potato Galette, Crème Fraîche, and Osetra Caviar 202
French Crumb Cake with Huckleberry Sauce 106
Furnace Creek Inn 191

G

Garlic Mashed Potatoes 56
Glendorn 41
Grand Canyon Lodge 153
Grand Canyon National Park 158
Grand Teton National Park 115
Granola Crème Brûlée 150
Granola, Zion Lodge 151
Great Smoky Mountains National Park 53